Breaking the Chain of
Low Self-Esteem

Praise for other books by
Marilyn J. Sorensen, Ph.D.

Low Self-Esteem Misunderstood & Misdiagnosed

"...outstanding resource. Sorensen expertly guides readers in self-evaluation. Author connects with readers, has excellent writing skills, establishes warm, comfortable tone."
— **TODAY'S LIBRARIAN**

"carefully explains...why [low self-esteem] is seldom recognized or treated seriously...This is an important book that could save lives."
— **THE STATESMAN JOURNAL**

"...candid, straight forward...an excellent book, specifically for people who've tried to seek help and found nothing useful. Highly Recommended."
— **THE MIDWEST BOOK REVIEW**

"I am a clinician and am just completing your book...I will want more training in this area as it is clear to me how misdiagnoses occur..."
— **Lisa Rathbun, MSW, CSW, OTR**

The Personal Workbook for Breaking the Chain of Low Self-Esteem

"Her open, clear approach and plain language cut to the heart of things and help readers make their way through some very upsetting realizations."
— **THE STATESMAN JOURNAL**

"Dr. Sorensen's words on developing healthy self-esteem are as wise as they are practical."
— **Ed Johnson, Host & Producer, OPB**

The Handbook for Building Healthy Self-Esteem in Children

"*The Handbook for Building Healthy Self-Esteem In Children* is a fantastic resource for adults who care about children. Implementation of its practical, effective, easy-to-understand tools and methods will foster a healthy self-concept in our children that can protect them from risky behavior and help them grow into their full selves.
— **Kathy Masarie, M.D., Founder and Program Director of Full Esteem Ahead**

Low Self-Esteem In The Bedroom

"Dr. Sorensen has done it again! Since her ground-breaking book, *Breaking the Chain of Low Self-Esteem*, where she demonstrated that LSE is the true source of most psychological problems including depression, anxiety, and social phobia, she now carries her thesis further in *Low Self-Esteem in the Bedroom*, where she explains that LSE is also the critical factor in developing and maintaining intimacy."
— **Robert Ludlow, M.D., Psychiatrist, Specialist in Sexual Medicine; Faculty, Cinncinnati Psychological Institute**

"Using the same powerful combination of clinical insight and real life examples that were used so effectively in her initial work of *Breaking the Chain of Low Self-Esteem*, Dr. Sorensen has created the best book I've ever read about intimacy that leads to true sexual intimacy."
— **Karl Pister, LCSW, Portland, OR, The Coaching Group, Inc.**

Available in bookstores nationwide
or at a discount through www.TheSelfEsteemInstitute.com

The Self-Esteem Recovery Toolkit

Materials designed to help LSE sufferers continue their individual daily process of recovering from low self-esteem.

The Toolkit is only available through the website:
www.TheSelfEsteemInstitute.com

Breaking the Chain of Low Self-Esteem

Marilyn J Sorensen, PhD

Wolf Publishing Co.
Sherwood, OR 97140

BREAKING THE CHAIN OF LOW SELF-ESTEEM
SECOND EDITION

Editor: Jill Kelly, Ph.D.
Cover and Page Layout: Anita Jones, Another Jones Graphics
Indexer: Carol Rappleyea
Photographer: Julie Theberge, Portraits by Design

Library of Congress Catalog Number: 2006902785

First Printing, June 2006
10   9   8   7   6   5   4   3   2   1

ISBN 10: 0-9664315-8-8
ISBN 13: 978-9664315-8-2
Printed in the United States of America

Wolf Publishing Co.
16890 SW Daffodil St.
Sherwood, OR 97140

Acknowledgements

Sandra K. Pinches, Ph.D., my dear friend and colleague. How do I sufficiently thank you for your unwavering belief in my ideas and this book? You gave me the initial momentum and courage to begin; you spent endless hours reading and discussing my material; and you gave me support and encouragement to "take a break" or "keep going" when it was needed. Through it all, you have been my mainstay. My heartfelt thanks, Sande!

Jill Kelly, Ph.D., my great editor, (a) whose expertise helped me get back into writing after so many years' layoff, (b) who patiently read and reread my material and announced one day, "You've found your voice, Marilyn," and (c) who has become my friend and chief supporter. Thanks, Jill—I'm so glad I found you.

Anita Jones, on whom I depend so much to layout my manuscripts in a professional, interesting, and readable fashion. Thank you, Anita, for being so dependable and reliable and for becoming my friend. Your efforts have greatly contributed to the success of my work.

In loving memory of
my mother, Violet Belle (Day) Sorensen
my father, Aage James Sorensen
my grandmother, Maren Sorensen

and my "children"
Kazan
Shaun

Contents

Preface

In recent years, many of us have become intensely interested in human behavior—both our own and that of those around us. In pursuing this interest, we have developed an awareness of social issues like harassment, battering, domestic violence, and other forms of abuse, and we ponder why people behave as they do. Searching for answers to this perplexing question, we have come face to face with our own unresolved pain and our unhappiness. We realize that we haven't understood ourselves or recognized the sources of our problems. We now look for ways to cope; some days we struggle just to keep going, while continuing in our quest to find peace and happiness.

We have become avid readers; volumes of new self-help books are available to quench our thirst. We have been encouraged to examine the dysfunctional family, shame, and codependency from every angle, with the result that many of us are now receiving guidance and experiencing some relief. While these approaches may have provided partial understanding and new insights, many still feel that *no one has fully addressed the problems they struggle with* or *discovered the core of their conflicts.* Thus peace, happiness and fulfillment continue to be elusive.

In my work as a psychologist, I have discovered patterns of behavior that clarify the root cause of most of the pain and discomfort people continue to experience. Based on thousands of psychotherapeutic hours spent with people struggling to free themselves from inner conflict, I have concluded that a *severe and often disabling state of low self-esteem (LSE) is the culprit.* Although many books and articles have been written about self-esteem and the term has become a household word, I believe that we have not yet recognized how profoundly LSE affects us.

Many people now identify LSE as one source of their struggles. Teachers and parents seeking to explain children's problems have frequently labeled the enemy low self-esteem. Magazines and newspapers, recognizing the recent surge of interest, have featured articles about how low self-esteem affects both children and adults. With information more readily available, people are beginning to understand the many ways low self-esteem influences their behavior and impinges on their lives *although few grasp its full impact.*

Since you are drawn to this book, *the subject must hold interest for you, too.* You may be among those discovering that you are plagued by low self-esteem but feel you need more information. You may actually have been wrestling with fear and anxiety related to LSE for some time but desperately feel the need for guidance in addressing it. You may have a loved one whom you suspect has low self-esteem but may be unaware of any way to help. Whatever the reason for your interest, you obviously want to know more about self-esteem. *This book will provide you with that information.*

This book presents a guideline for understanding the effects of low self-esteem in life and offers insights in approaching the problem. Numerous examples, observations, and explanations provide a new understanding and a plan for alleviating the lingering pain that accompanies low self-esteem. Addressing the five points below, this book will give you a fresh approach to gaining peace and satisfaction in your life.

This book will address the formidable foe of low self-esteem in five ways.

- You will acquire a vivid picture of exactly what low self-esteem is and how it developed in you.

- You will learn the various ways self-esteem plays out on a daily basis and discover how it interferes with, and negatively impacts, nearly every aspect of life.

You will increase your awareness of how low self-esteem *may presently be affecting your own choices and actions.*

- You will develop an understanding of the basic dysfunctional behavior patterns common among those with low self-esteem.

- You will recognize that *there is hope* in alleviating the effects of low self-esteem.

- You will receive direction on how to begin to tackle the problem.

In over twenty years of observing clients' behavior, I have found that many of my clients repeatedly engage in certain very similar patterns of thinking and behavior. Continuing to seek understanding for the pain, anxiety, and despair of these individuals, I realized that most of these feelings related to low self-esteem. As I then began to understand the complex inner logic that was the basis of their behavior, I developed steps toward clarifying the dysfunctional pattern: a new method for treating the problem.

As therapy continued and clients gained new insights, I saw them make constructive changes, fully engaged in the battle to subdue and destroy the enemy that was controlling and damaging their lives. Sharing in their fight to overcome emotional distress and extreme unhappiness, I developed a deep respect for them. Indeed, I found I liked them and greatly admired their perseverance in searching for solutions and mechanisms of change.

Many of these individuals had seen numerous therapists over a long period of time and felt they had received little or no help. Many felt they had been misdiagnosed and treated as if they were mentally ill. The consensus seemed to be that their former therapists appeared perplexed about the goal of therapy. At times, the therapists had seemed irritated, even hostile. Predictably, these clients felt even more hopeless when they experienced what they perceived as rejection from their therapists; they left these therapists feeling skeptical about therapy, alienated, more hopeless, misunderstood, and deeply hurt. Perhaps these therapists did not fully understand the complexities and pervasive effects of low self-esteem.

In addition, therapists sometimes do not recognize that LSE is a client's primary problem. Low self-esteem shares characteristics with many other diagnosable problems, while not completely fitting any of these other categories. For example, a person may enter therapy complaining of depression, when it is really an effect of low self-esteem. Dealing with the depression will merely mean working with a symptom—not the actual problem. The therapist must be careful, therefore, to get a complete picture of the person's concerns, rather than relying only on the initial complaint of depression. Only with this kind of careful observation can the therapist identify the subtleties that differentiate LSE from other diagnoses. When low self-esteem is not recognized and treated as the core issue, it defies intervention, leaving both therapist and client frustrated with the lack of progress. One should, therefore, select a therapist with a deep and thorough understanding of this specific problem.

Therapists routinely try to match a client's problems and complaints with accepted diagnostic categories, but there is no category for low self-esteem in diagnostic manuals. The American Psychiatric Association's reason for not including it deserves clarification. It is true that a long history of disagreement between psychiatrists and psychologists does exist. Were LSE to be given a diagnostic category, *it would not, in most instances, necessitate the services of a psychiatrist* and would probably become the chosen diagnosis for many clients who now see psychiatrists. One can only wonder if that influences the decision.

With no category available to diagnose self-esteem problems, insurance carriers can avoid covering what is probably the largest mental health problem that exists—the suffering of those with LSE. Therapists are unlikely to specialize in an area that will require clients to pay out of pocket, knowing that many will be unable to do so.

Finding a therapist to work with issues of low self-esteem is difficult for another reason. In recent years, the majority of therapists have succumbed to the dictates of managed care; they have altered their therapy to align themselves with the demands of the insurance companies. These companies favor therapists who confine their practices to short-term therapy—the only type of therapy for which managed care will pay, enabling the insurers to pay less money in benefits. Managed care companies will not knowingly enroll, and will soon eliminate from their panels, therapists who provide long-term therapy. These time limitations do not work when one is dealing with issues of low self-esteem. *Instead, long-term therapy is not only the therapy of choice but also the essential therapy for this problem—there can be no substitute.*

The person seeking help for LSE may wonder why long-term therapy is so strongly endorsed. Consider that the problems associated with low self-esteem have generally developed over an entire life, beginning in childhood. Dysfunctional habits have been formed and are deeply entrenched. Therapy, which generally consists of a fifty-minute session once or twice a week, must then deal with removing this lifetime of well-established dysfunctional patterns while offering unfamiliar alternatives to the client. This indicates that no "quick fix" will work; instead, the person will have to acquire new skills, change old attitudes, and develop a new perspective—all of which takes considerable time.

My intention in saying all of this is certainly not to discourage you but rather to inform you and prepare you to work diligently toward fulfillment. While healing from past wounds that have caused the low self-esteem may not come quickly, it is attainable. And while self-esteem can never be fully restored to its original potential, it can be repaired and become fully operational, allowing for a meaningful and happy life.

■

In this book, we walk though life with "Jane," a woman who deals daily with extremely low self-esteem. We become acquainted with her emotions, her actions and reactions, her thinking processes, her relationships: in essence, her general state of mind. We hear about the environment she has come from, the motivation for her present behavior, her daily struggles to cope, and her goals for the future. We witness her tears and her fears, her frustration and her desperation, her anxiety and her misery.

As we read, we learn what it means to look at life through the eyes of someone with devastatingly low self-esteem.

Jane is an intelligent woman, age 39, divorced, and with no children. She is pleasantly attractive, neat and well groomed, though not particularly stylish. She works as a marketing development specialist and department head for a large corporation that manufactures athletic equipment. She has worked there for 12 years, beginning four years after graduation from college. She was in the process of divorcing her husband, John, when she began working for this company. She has received four promotions and has been in her present position for nearly three years.

■

Please note that Jane is a fictional character; she is not a client, acquaintance, or friend. She is, however, very real in that she represents the typical person suffering from extremely low self-esteem. If you, too, suffer from low self-esteem, you will probably see yourself in Jane—you may recognize the thought patterns, the behavior patterns, the expectations and responses she gives. You may not identify with all the examples, but you may see yourself in enough of them to realize that you, too, are encumbered with low self-esteem. This book was written to start you on the road to recovery from this nagging problem through the first step: awareness. Acquiring awareness of what LSE is and how it so negatively affects lives is a huge step towards understanding and then beginning to move out of the quagmire.

1

Low Self-Esteem: What Is It?

Low Self-Esteem: Believing that I am inadequate (flawed),
unworthy, unlovable, and/or incompetent

JANE: a negative view of herself

*When Jane's divorce became final, she began working in
the marketing department of a large corporation that manufactures athletic equipment. Though reeling from her failed marriage, she had been forced to seek immediate employment and
had been fortunate to find a good job. When the time came for
her first yearly review, Jane worried about how her evaluation
would go. She was filled with self-doubt and self-recrimination
due both to her divorce and her parents' critical child-rearing
practices.*

*As the review began, she listened quietly as her manager
pointed out what she considered to be Jane's strengths and listed
several specific projects in which she felt Jane had performed far
above expectations. Assigning Jane the labels of "valued
employee" and "quick study," the manager praised Jane for her*

initiative, creativity, and responsible work ethic and noted that a raise would be forthcoming. Jane was cautiously pleased; she couldn't keep from smiling, albeit reservedly.

Next, the supervisor told Jane that she did have a few minor suggestions for improvement. Jane's eyes narrowed, her smile slackened. As her department head briefly mentioned the specific recommendations, Jane's chest began to feel heavy, her eyelids began to droop, and she could feel her heart pounding. With tears welling up behind her eyelids, she heard the all-too-familiar word "failure" spoken by the voice in her head; she felt devastated.

Seeing that Jane was becoming upset by her few words of constructive criticism, Jane's supervisor reiterated that the company was extremely pleased with her overall performance. Jane nodded, feeling embarrassed that her supervisor was trying to comfort her, not believing the positive feedback. She just wanted the review to end—she wanted to flee. Pasting a smile on her face, she whispered a thank you and scurried out of the office. By the time she reached her desk, Jane could not remember the words of praise and approval but only the criticism. Condemning self-statements flooded her mind, this time at the volume of a bullhorn. She felt exhausted and stared at the clock, desperately willing it to move faster so it would be time to go home. Jane, who has low self-esteem, was suffering from a self-esteem attack.

Like each of us, Jane has a picture in her head that she believes represents who she is, a very personal view by which she measures her worth, her competence, her worthiness, and her ability to cope and succeed in life. This picture is subjective because it is implanted in her head alone; it's "her" view, based on "her" own perspective. It may not be the perception of others who know her, and it may not be accurate, but this view of herself has everything to do with the ways in which she approaches or avoids life, with the ways in which she acts and reacts, and how she shapes her hopes for the future. Like Jane, this view of self is the basis for how all of us perceive, value, or esteem ourselves—it represents our self-esteem.

Furthermore, because Jane's picture of herself is based primarily or entirely on negative interpretations of past experiences, she believes that she is less worthy or less competent than others and labels herself as such. It is this negative view of self that produces low self-esteem (LSE).

How is This Negative View Formed?

As we go through life, we record our memories and our interpretations, though not necessarily the facts surrounding those memories. From these countless recollections, we have the makings of a movie of our life. Jane thinks in much the same way a VCR works—it rewinds and replays past events. This analogy can help explain how she has formed her views of herself and how that view is the basis for her behavior.

Families and their environments

A child's view of herself begins to form as soon as she is born. Based on the things she is told, the specific situations she experiences, and how she is treated, a picture of her "self" evolves. If she is praised and encouraged, she likely begins to develop healthy self-esteem; if, however, she is consistently criticized, ridiculed, or told she can't do things right, she begins to question her competency and adequacy. If her feelings are ignored, she begins to feel unimportant; if she is shamed, she starts to feel unworthy. (More about childhood factors leading to low self-esteem can be found in Chapter 7).

Jane was raised in an environment that caused her to doubt her adequacy and her competence when she was just a child. Discouraging remarks, ridicule, and criticism set the stage for the movie of her life in which the stinging bite of her parents' disapproval remained a key influence. Desperately needing their support and affirmation, Jane struggled to prove her self-worth by excelling in music, sports, and scholastics, but she experienced countless situations that told her she was not good enough. The scars remain and now, still confused and filled with doubt, she continues to evaluate herself on the basis of these numerous past incidents, especially when she again receives criticism.

JANE: as a teenager

When Jane was a child, she felt she could never win the approval of her parents no matter how hard she tried. When she was thirteen, her parents traveled across the country to attend a funeral, leaving her and her brother Paul, who was sixteen, alone at home for a week. The morning before they were to return, the two children decided they would surprise their parents by thoroughly cleaning the house—something they had never done by themselves. Turning down invitations from their friends, they vacuumed, dumped the trash, cleaned their bedroom, tidied the living room, washed and put away all the dishes. They even mopped the kitchen floor and cleaned the bathroom. They could hardly wait until their parents arrived, to see their surprised faces; they just knew their parents would be proud to see their children had become so responsible.

When their parents came home, they came in through the back door. Jane's mother walked by the laundry area and looked in. There on the floor lay a pile of rags that Jane and Paul had forgotten to wash. She yelled at her two children to come to her.

When they appeared, she scolded them and asked why they had left such a mess on the floor. Paul was disappointed and Jane was devastated. They looked at each other and Paul shrugged; Jane retreated to her room. A few minutes later their mother asked, "Where's Jane? We want to hear about your week and we have some things for both of you." "She's upset that you didn't notice we cleaned the whole house," Paul replied. "Well, I haven't had time to notice," his mother said. To himself, Paul thought, "She sure had time to notice the one mess we made."

The negative comments from Jane's mother coupled with the absence of any positive ones led Jane to believe that the mistake they had made (leaving the rags on the floor) was all that mattered, that that mistake discounted or invalidated the much larger accomplishment of cleaning the entire house. Her achievement was ignored and her mistake magnified. What Jane learned from this and many similar incidents was that anything less than perfection proves you are inadequate, a message repeated by her father, as in the following example.

JANE: as an athlete

When Jane was sixteen and a member of the community girls' softball team, her parents attended one of her games. On this particular evening, Jane, who was a top athlete, came to bat four times, hitting three home runs and striking out once. She was thrilled. No one she had ever known had hit three home runs in one game.

After the game, she was excited to see her parents. They must be proud; maybe they would finally tell her so. With a big grin on her face, she ran up the bleachers where they were seated and blurted out, "Well, how did I do?"

"How about that, three homers!" Her father said; then he leaned over and quietly whispered, "But I can't believe you struck out." Jane's heart sank. Tears came to her eyes. She sat as if frozen for a few seconds, then she said, "Gotta go," turned away, and ran down the bleachers. She looked for a place to hide, tears streaming down her face.

Both of Jane's parents tended to be negative, though Jane's mother more consistently so. Not wanting her to become too proud or complacent, they unknowingly tried to motivate her through criticism, pointing out her failures. They complimented her, but their practice of always adding a criticism plunged Jane into bouts of depression mingled with rage. She felt she could never do enough or do it right. At times she felt as if she hated them and at other times she thought that there must be something wrong with her, that maybe she was just unlovable.

Jane's view of herself has been constructed from the editing of billions of video sequences like those above, sequences that her built-in camcorder—her eyes and brain—has recorded throughout her life and then relegated to "memory." Jane's video, therefore, consists of her own memories of past incidents, circumstances, and behavior—both words and actions—that make up her life. All of us have a similar video.

This video production is with Jane at all times and is only a thought away. Programmed to rerun on her mental screen instantaneously and without conscious request, it does not require fast forwarding or rewinding to the exact spot. Instead, the video player can abruptly and without warning bring any memory or accompanying emotion into Jane's consciousness. These memories and emotions include her interpretations of any relevant incident, interpretations that may or may not be accurate.

For instance, Jane may believe that her mother doesn't love her; this may or may not be true. Her mother may, in fact, love Jane but be emotionally unstable, have low self-esteem herself, lack parenting skills, or have some other problem. Because of the negative reactions of both her parents, however, Jane may conclude that the fault lies within her, that there is something basically wrong with her, that she is unlovable, as mentioned above. She may doubt her abilities to play softball though she is an outstanding player, or she may decide to prove herself, devoting herself to becoming an even better player in an attempt to win their approval, approval that may never come. Jane may become angry because her parents are so critical, feeling defeated each time she accomplishes something but then is admonished in some way.

Life is the author of this particular video and Jane the featured star, but the potential problem is that she is the editor as well. As editor, she alone decides what is worth retaining in this video and what is to be ignored or deleted, what is relevant and what is not, what is truth and what is not. This, of course, means that it is not a true or objective documentary of the facts but rather a version based on Jane's perceptions and consequent interpretation of the past—her subjective view. Unable to point blame at her parents, Jane may believe things about herself that are not true. (Read more on this in Chapter 7.) Or if she becomes angry, she may become confused and wonder what is so wrong with her that they treat her this way.

Jane may select particular events for her video because she has assigned more importance to them, perhaps because they had a greater effect on her life than others she has deemed less significant. This could include positive events, such as when she won several scholarships to college, or negative, such as the one below.

JANE: second place

At the end of Jane's senior year in high school, the school superintendent called Jane and Lizzy into his office. He immediately began praising Lizzy for her scholastic achievement, which had earned her the honor of being Valedictorian of their class.

*Continuing to focus on Lizzy, he told her that she would be giv-
ing a speech at graduation and should limit her remarks to ten
minutes. Jane sat listening, waiting for him to compliment her
in similar fashion since she knew she was the Salutatorian.
When the superintendent finished talking to Lizzy, however, he
merely glanced at her and said, "Oh, and Jane, you took second
place. Your speech should be only three minutes long." Jane low-
ered her eyes to the floor; she felt totally deflated. Her excitement
was gone and she felt enraged. He was treating her as though her
accomplishment was nothing at all.*

Winning the scholarship tells Jane she is very intelligent while
remarks about her being "second place" insinuate that she is still
missing the mark, she is still inadequate.

Accordingly, specific emotions will accompany each of these
reflections or interpretations of such past events. Elation and
pride might accompany winning a scholarship, if we wanted to go
to college. Discouragement, doubt, and resentment might accompany the honor of being salutatorian when it is placed in a negative
light that insinuates that our accomplishment is insignificant.

With this in mind, what will Jane's video look like if she has
retained only the negative interpretation of all she has achieved,
when the feedback she has received always focused on how she
was lacking, on what she could have done better? How can she
sort through her successes and her failures when only the latter
have been accented? How can she have confidence in herself
when that certainty has been shaken time and again? How can she
believe she is a unique and significant being when her feelings have
been invalidated—when her sense of self has been pummeled? Will
Jane value her good grades, her performance in sports, her popular-
ity with her classmates, her awards, her musical talent in order to
determine who she is? Likely not. Or will her view of herself con-
verge around the disappointments, the criticism, the rebukes, the
neglect, the lack of approval, and the emotional abuse she has

received? The latter is, unfortunately, the more likely—partly because it comes from the people whose opinion she values most—her parents and other authority figures. Ultimately, from her interpretation of these memories, these lessons, these disappointments, and harsh words, Jane will form her picture of herself.

Do you see the problem?

- Jane's conditioned perceptions of herself are inaccurate.

- Jane's analysis, synthesis, and interpretation of these perceptions are, therefore, untrue.

- Jane's entire video is distorted.

- Jane's image of herself is based mainly on negative, inaccurate video sequences; it is skewed.

- Jane does not have high regard or esteem for the person presented in the video: herself. Instead, she has severely low self-esteem.

Like Jane, each of us possesses such a video. It is essential to our lives because it contains the storehouse of experience and knowledge that forms the basis of our attitudes, standards, beliefs, and values. Put to good use, this video enables us to review, to reminisce, to enjoy, to learn, and to utilize all that has gone on in our lives.

Those who have healthy self-esteem possess a video containing both positive and negative information. Because their backgrounds have been more uplifting, encouraging, accepting, and balanced, they have a means of evaluating, sorting, and utilizing this input in a way that is discriminating, fair, and accurate.

On the other hand, people with LSE initially have a video that contains both positive and negative sequences, but they have received such an inordinate amount of negative feedback that they tend to focus on the negative portions while editing out the positive ones as extraneous. For example, they shrug off praise or a compliment, or discount it, because they have been programmed to look for any way they are less than perfect. They seem to tightly grasp and even nurture the negative reruns so these memories actually grow in size and importance. Thus, the person with low self-esteem discards the positive while actually "enlarging" and "enhancing" those tape sequences containing unfavorable personal information. As he has been trained to do, the person focuses on his failures, weaknesses, unattained skills, and imperfections as though these were the only pieces of relevant, reliable information available. It is obvious how distorted the results are, yet consider then that these results are the basis for his self-esteem.

People who do this do not purposely distort reality. They are completely unaware that they have a faulty filtering system; they are merely computing information the way they have been taught to do so. They do not know that they process information differently from those with healthy self-esteem. Instead, they are convinced that their retrieval system is sound and that their conclusions about themselves are accurate. After all, this is the feedback they have received throughout their developmental years. They have lived their lives believing this learned assessment process is correct and have formed fixed beliefs about themselves as a result.

Example:

> *Zack, a high school music teacher with two music degrees, is asked to sing a solo for a community function. He is pleased at being asked and enjoys singing but gets very nervous, fearful he will make a mistake and embarrass himself. He considers himself an above-average vocalist by local standards but worries*

that people will expect him to be even better than he is because he teaches music and has studied it in college.

Zack sings his solo, aware that he has made two mistakes (they are actually minor mistakes, ones no one else could possibly be aware of.) After the meeting, several people approach Zack to compliment him on his solo. They are exuberant in their praise and Zack smiles, thanking them while inside feeling like a fraud. To himself he says, "They just don't realize that it wasn't as good as they think. If they were aware of my mistakes, they wouldn't be saying these things" or "They are just trying to make me feel good; they heard my mistakes." He feels humiliated and depressed.

People with LSE are experts at filtering out and nullifying positive input. Zack successfully sings his solo, but he has been taught that anything less than perfection constitutes an inadequate performance.

Those listening enjoy and appreciate his vocal presentation but Zack's filtering system discounts these compliments; instead, he focuses on the small errors he has made and feels bad about himself. People with LSE are usually adept at finding ways to turn positive feedback into negative as shown in the following incident.

Example:

Sihieb recognizes that his girlfriend, Minnie, is very insecure. Consequently, he consciously tries to tell her the things that he likes and admires about her.

One evening when he comes to pick her up, he realizes she has an attractive new hair cut and tells her so effusively, "Wow, Min, I really like your hair. You look great." Minnie blushes in embarrassment. She wonders if he is really telling her that he didn't like the way it looked before.

People with low self-esteem have believed the worst about themselves so strongly and for so long that they readily discard any feedback that contradicts their belief. They are unable to trust compliments and praise and often unknowingly twist such comments to mean the opposite. Overly self-conscious, they are easily embarrassed when they are the center of attention.

When those with low self-esteem are told that their process of self-evaluation is unrealistically negative and inaccurate, they do not believe it. When they are reminded of other information that contradicts their negative view, they find a way to discount that information; the suggestion that the way they judge themselves might be incorrect is difficult for them to digest. How can they contemplate that the view they have of themselves might not be true, a view upon which they have based their lives? To consider that he has been incorrect all these years is equivalent to asking a religious person to question the tenets that are the foundation for his life, or proposing to a staunch, politically active Democrat that she become a Republican. This recommendation is beyond consideration. Suggesting to the person with LSE that she has based her life decisions on distorted interpretations is equally incomprehensible. This is the enduring and unyielding nature of the dysfunction of low self-esteem.

Who Suffers from Low Self-Esteem?

We may think that those who have LSE are the down-and-out, unsuccessful in their careers and their relationships. This is not necessarily true, for people with low self-esteem are present in all walks of life. They are executives, professionals, entrepreneurs, laborers, skilled workers, teachers, clerks, beauticians, in fact, people from all occupations. They are highly educated and minimally educated. They are male and female, old and young, wealthy and poor; they are single, coupled, and divorced; they are of all nationalities. They include the religious, the atheist, and the agnostic. They reside in cities, in suburbs, and in rural areas. Some seek therapy; some do not. Some are aware they have low self-esteem; many are not.

Altering the detrimental and lasting effects of low self-esteem requires several distinct skills. When you are finished reading this book, you will be able to:

- Recognize why you now have low self-esteem.

- Identify the negative effects of low self-esteem in your life.

- Recognize the reactions you have that are related to low self-esteem.

- Understand how these reactions impact your life in self-defeating ways, possibly on a daily basis.

- Identify your specific behavior patterns and distinguish what needs to be changed.

- Identify new, constructive behaviors that can replace old, harmful ones.

- Formulate strategies you can use to battle low self-esteem.

- Begin to build your life anew!

After you recognize the new behaviors you need to acquire, your task will be to:

- Practice, practice, practice these new behaviors.

- Seek help, if you feel you cannot do it on your own.

SORENSEN SELF-ESTEEM TEST

Place a check next to the number of each statement that you find to be true.

1. ✓ I generally feel anxious in new social situations where I may not know what is expected of me.

2. ___ I find it difficult to hear criticism about myself.

3. ___ I fear being made to look like a fool.

4. ✓ I tend to magnify my mistakes and minimize my successes.

5. ✓ I am very critical of myself and others.

6. ___ I have periods in which I feel devastated and/or depressed.

7. ___ I am anxious and fearful much of the time.

8. ___ When someone mistreats me, I think that I must have done something to deserve it.

9. ✓ I have difficulty knowing whom to trust and when to trust.

10. ___ I often feel like I don't know the right thing to do or say.

11. ✓ I am very concerned about my appearance.

12. ___ I am easily embarrassed.

13. ✓ I think others are very focused on—and critical of—what I say and do.

14. ___ I fear making a mistake which others might see.

15. ___ I often feel depressed about things I've said and done, or things I failed to say or do.

16. ___ I have avoided making changes in my life because I was fearful of making a mistake or failing.

17. ___ I often get defensive and strike back when I perceive I am being criticized.

18. ___ I have not accomplished what I am capable of due to fear and avoidance.

19. ___ I tend to let fear and anxiety control many of my decisions.

20. ___ I tend to think negatively much of the time.

21. ___ I have found it difficult to perform adequately or without embarrassment when involved in sex.

22. ___ I'm one of the following: The person who reveals too much personal information about myself or the person who seldom reveals personal information.

23. ___ I often get so anxious that I don't know what to say.

24. ___ I often procrastinate.

25. ___ I try to avoid conflict and confrontation.

26. ___ I've been told I'm too sensitive.

27. ___ I felt inferior or inadequate as a child.

28. ___ I tend to think that I have higher standards than others.

29. ___ I often feel like I don't know what is expected of me.

30. ___ I often compare myself to others.

31. ___ I frequently think negative thoughts about myself and others.

32. ___ I often feel that others mistreat me and or take advantage of me.

33. ___ At night, I frequently review my day, analyzing what I said and did or what others said and did to me that day.

34. ___ I often make decisions on the basis of what would please others rather than on what I want or without even considering what I want.

35. ___ I often think that others don't respect me.

36. ___ I often refrain from sharing my opinions, my ideas, and my feelings in groups.

37. ___ I sometimes lie when I feel that the truth would result in criticism or rejection.

38. ___ I'm fearful that I will say or do something that will make me look stupid or incompetent.

39. ___ I do not set goals for the future.

40. ___ I am easily discouraged.

41. ___ I am not very aware of my feelings.

42. ___ I grew up in a dysfunctional home.

43. ___ I think life is harder for me than for most other people.

44. ___ I often avoid situations where I think I will be uncomfortable.

45. ___ I tend to be a perfectionist, needing to look perfect and to do things perfectly.

46. ___ I feel too embarrassed to eat out alone or to attend movies and other activities by myself.

47. ___ I often find myself angry or hurt by the behavior and words of others.

48. ___ At times I get so anxious or upset that I experience most of the following: heart racing or pounding, sweating; tearfulness; blushing; difficulty swallowing or lump in my throat; shaking; poor concentration dizziness, nausea or diarrhea; butterflies.

49. ___ I am very fearful of criticism, disapproval, or rejection.

50. ___ I rely on the opinion of others to make decisions.

If you checked:
00-04 Statements:......................You have fairly good self-esteem
05-10 Statements:........................You have mild low self-esteem
11-18 Statements:...............You have moderately low self-esteem
19-50 Statements:...................You have severely low self-esteem

It's important to realize that your score on this questionnaire in no way indicates that you are not a quality person. Instead what it does is to measure how you view yourself.

If you have a healthy view of yourself, your score will be low. If your view of yourself is unhealthy, your score will be high.

Be aware that it will be difficult to raise children with healthy self-esteem if you yourself suffer from low self-esteem. Without realizing it, you will pass on the attitudes, fears, and thinking that accompany low self-esteem.

RECOVERY

While our situations in life vary, we each have the capacity to alter the course of our lives. We have the ability to become the captain of our own ship, the person who controls the transitions in our lives. We can take steps that will result in restored hope, stimulated motivation, and renewed confidence: steps that will guarantee a fresh outlook for the future and a new outcome for our lives. We can attain skills not yet mastered; we can learn to face our fears; we can set fresh, fulfilling goals and acquire the means to reach those goals. We do not have to continue being held captive by the chain of low self-esteem.

What is required is a desire to change, a longing and willingness to put focused energy into recovering from the devastating effects of LSE. Some will see this need to change as a challenge, a roadblock that impedes their movement but one they can dislodge; for others, this need to change will represent an insurmountable blockade. In truth, we all have the capacity to change if we want it badly enough. It is a choice. Those who do not opt to work toward change will once again be choosing self-defeating behaviors over those that can enhance and better their lives; they will be choosing to remain stifled, enslaved, and miserable. Those who choose to work at improving their lives, who actively work at improving their self-esteem, will reap the rewards; each step towards recovery will break one link in the chain of low self-esteem.

The author recommends that you purchase and use a notebook while reading this book. Many of the exercises suggest that you jot down your responses, thoughts, and other relevant information. She also suggests that you write down any feelings or memories that come to mind as you go through the book.

THINGS TO DO

Exercise 1

This book contains suggestions throughout that are designed to help you to: (a) become more aware of how you see yourself and (b) to recognize why those negative thinking patterns are irrational and untrue. (This book is the first step in my 3-step plan for recovery.)

If you recognize that you have low self-esteem but question why or what to do about it, try doing these exercises. Do not expect to accomplish them in a week or a month. Take your time and work as you feel you can. (Purchase or use a new notebook that is reserved entirely for your personal work, so you can save it and review it as necessary.)

Developing awareness of the factors in our lives that may have contributed to our picture of ourselves is important. As we become conscious of the situations and conditions that have formed our negative view of self, we will be better prepared to sort out the reality of who we really are. Many people do not realize that they come from dysfunctional backgrounds because it is all they know or have experienced—they have nothing to compare it to. As adults, however, we are more equipped to sort out the truth of our early years, possibly even including the fact that we were emotionally or otherwise abused. Recognizing this may then cast a new light on all of the perceptions we have of ourselves and alter the interpretations of what we have learned.

This is an exercise that many balk at doing. They do not want to think negatively about their parents or other authority figures; they do not want to focus on unhappiness. Yet this willingness to evaluate the past is essential to understanding why we feel the way we do—why we picture ourselves in such a negative light—and it is necessary for overcoming low self-esteem (LSE).

Make four columns in your notebook. At the top, title column 1 Positive, column 2 Negative, column 3 Feelings, and column 4 Person.

1. Think of 5 to 10 experiences from your childhood that you feel shaped your view of yourself—your self-esteem. This may be painful. Take your time. The more examples you can think of, the better.

2. Place a brief description of each significant experience in either the positive or negative column.

3. Identify the specific feelings (as best as you can remember) that you had immediately following each event, e.g., sad, happy, deflated, discouraged, encouraged, angry. If your list includes many examples where you were neglected, shown disapproval, criticized, or ridiculed, you may have identified a source of your low self-esteem. Place these descriptors in column 3.

4. List the people who were involved in your memories. Who are they? Are there different people in each situation, or is the same person or persons present in most of them? Place their names in column 4 behind each experience.

Now that you have completed the exercise, think about how these events and people contributed to the view you have of yourself. Do you see any patterns in how you were treated or how you responded that might have been destructive to your view of yourself? Could it be that the people who were most destructive in your life actually had problems of their own that were projected on to you—that they may have been too strict, too critical, too demanding of you? Can you see that the picture you have of yourself may not be accurate?

This is often difficult to comprehend and digest. Don't expect too much the first time you try this exercise. It is best if you have someone to talk through these findings with—a friend, sibling, or therapist. Getting their feedback and support and hearing some of their experiences can be very helpful.

THINGS TO DO

Exercise 2

Because our view of the past can only be from one perspective, it may be slanted, distorted, or inaccurate. We may not remember or even have noticed important details; we may have been too young to comprehend the significance of specific events. Talking to others who were present can often yield additional insight and clarity to our memories; such input from others can often verify our conclusions, add missing data to our questioning, and help repudiate our self-doubts. If possible, therefore, try this exercise.

If you have siblings, talk to them about your childhood.

1. Ask what they remember about the environment in which you grew up.

2. Reminisce about your shared childhood.

3. Ask questions you may have. Find out if they remember situations or incidents in the same way you do.

4. Ask them how they feel about themselves now. What struggles have they had? Notice if those struggles are similar to yours.

5. Jot down significant similarities or any additional insights gained from this experience.

People can grow up in the same home and feel very differently about their past for a variety of reasons. Often the youngest child experienced a very different environment than that of the eldest due to the economic changes in their parents' lives as well as educational and maturational ones. In addition, adults looking back

on their earlier years may have perceived that period of time differently because of their own ability to be introspective, their present
emotional state, or their own issues. If your siblings do not remember events as you do, do not take this to mean that your experiences are invalid; you may remember unique negative situations
that your siblings did not endure. This exercise is meant to give
you additional information and insight, not to cause you further
self-doubt.

2

Facing Fear and Anxiety

JANE: her marriage to John

Jane met her husband, John, when she was in graduate school and he was in law school. When they began dating, John had found it difficult to schedule time with Jane in advance. His homework required long tedious hours of study that made his free time unpredictable. Fearful that having found John, she might not be able to hold on to him, Jane became nervous when she did not see him regularly.

When John needed to take a break from studying for a few hours, he would usually call Jane, expecting her to be available to join him for a walk or lunch. Realizing she would only see him consistently if she were available when he called, she gradually gave up her exercise club, her softball team and, one by one, her friends.

They married immediately following John's graduation and Jane expected that he, too, would now want to spend all of his time with her. When, instead, he began to expand his interests and activities with his male friends, Jane felt that she was becoming less important to him.

Jane became progressively more insecure in their relation-ship until she rarely thought of anything else but John. Plagued with doubts about her own worth, she vowed over and over to prove to John that she was the perfect wife. John's reactions, however, did not alleviate her fears. He seemed pleased with her efforts, complimented her cooking and other accomplishments, but also encouraged her to spend time with her friends. He even suggested she get a job, which Jane interpreted as his way of try-ing to push her away. Why else would he want her to develop more of a life away from him?

Near despair that she was losing John, Jane frantically attempted to rein him in and control his time with others. John, noticing how demanding and dependent she had become, began criticizing her, telling her she was nagging him all the time, even though he was equally demanding in other ways.

After three years of marriage, John announced to Jane that he was seeking a divorce. Jane was shocked to actually hear her worst fears put into words. She was numb and later furious. How dare he choose to leave her when she had devoted herself totally to him for all this time! She decided he was discarding her now that his career was moving forward!

Terrified, Jane wondered what she would do. John had been her whole life. Overwhelmed by fear, she wondered if she could take care of herself. How he could do this to her? She concluded that her mother had been right. She just couldn't do things right—she couldn't even keep her husband—she was a failure.

Fear and anxiety are driving forces in the life of an individual with low self-esteem. Although a person like Jane may have great strength and energy, the emotions that accompany LSE divert her efforts into a self-defeating cycle of behavior. For example, Jane's fear of rejection was so great it prompted her to act in ways that destroyed the very thing she wanted: her marriage. The frequency and degree to which fear drives a person's reactions reflects the severity of her low self-esteem. Also, the strategies used to manage these fears tend to be more or less functional, depending on the relative amounts of affirmation and negation the person has experienced.

All individuals with LSE experience fear and anxiety stemming from their belief that they are inadequate and incompetent in one or more areas of their lives. Furthermore, they worry that at any moment they may unknowingly reveal their defects to the world and, in the process, bring criticism, disapproval, and rejection upon themselves. From past experience, they know that they respond to others' disapproval with extreme emotions, ranging from embarrassment to humiliation, devastation, and despair. When these feelings descend upon them, people with LSE feel overwhelmed and out of control. Whether or not the person is truly inadequate or incompetent in some way is irrelevant. Whether or not others really see her as such is also immaterial. What counts is that she believes it about herself and that she also believes that it is only a matter of time before she is "found out" by others. She believes that when this happens, she will suffer uncontrollably. Her negative expectations then lead her to protect herself in ways that bring the feared results.

For the person with LSE, the potential threat of revealing her inadequacy lurks at every corner, in each new experience and at any time that she is not on guard. This perspective makes daily life a potential battleground and the world a dangerous enemy.

The Four Specific Fears Accompanying Low Self-Esteem

Fears accompanying LSE fall into four categories, some or all of which are experienced by individuals with LSE. The worse the person's self-esteem, the more intense and numerous are the fears.

1. Fear of confirming one's own inadequacies.

People with low self-esteem fear doing something that will confirm what they already think is true—that they are, in fact, inadequate, unlovable, and inferior to others. Lacking confidence in themselves, they may see success as illusive and unattainable or they may feel successful in one area of their lives but fear trying anything new or different. They may, in fact, be quite successful but still doubt their adequacy.

Example:

Dale grew up in a home where his parents scoffed at his ideas and plans for the future. His father, a bitter retired salesman, repeatedly told Dale that he was "high and mighty" and thought he was too good for them. Now he tells his son that he had better stay and concentrate on his job as deliveryman because he isn't going to get anything better.

Though Dale hates his job, where the pay is poor and benefits are nonexistent, he is afraid to look for other work. Remembering his father's words, he wonders if this is truly all he is capable of. He worries that if he applies for a job, he won't know how to act or what to say during the interview. He fears that he might become tongue-tied or draw a blank when asked questions. Though he has a college degree, he wonders if

he could do another more demanding job. Deciding he would
probably be wasting his time and fearful that he will only be
confirming his inadequacy, he does not even look for a better job.

Dale, like others with LSE, has doubts about his competence
and feels unworthy; he has been told throughout his life that he
should settle for whatever he can get and not expect too much.
Dale is unable to recognize that his father is basing his negative
evaluation of his son on his own disappointment and bitterness—
caused by his own feelings of inadequacy.

If people with healthy self-esteem do not land a specific job,
they do not immediately conclude that one job rejection necessarily implies something about their competence; rather they understand that others more qualified may have applied for the job:
while disappointed, they move on looking for other jobs to apply
for. People with LSE, however, are overly aware of all disappointments and evaluate these very personally. They believe that the
negative circumstances in their lives are in some way a reflection
of their lack of worth and their incompetence as well as a man-
date for the future.

Consequently, the person with moderate to severe LSE is "on
alert" much of the time, waiting, watching, and ultimately avoiding any situation that might reveal some deficiency in him. Like
Dale, he does not apply for a new job, thinking his efforts will
prove to be futile and he will feel worse later. He becomes hyper-
vigilant in his efforts to predict and prepare for such threatening
situations, hoping to avoid doing anything that will confirm his
worst fears, cause him more grief, or cause him embarrassment in
front of others. He remains static; he resigns himself to staying in
his present boring job and avoids any new challenges in life.

He may be so anxious about new and unpredictable situations
that he prepares excuses that enable him to decline invitations. He
may look for places where he can retreat and hide to avoid the
event and to recover, if necessary. He may lie without hesitation

if he thinks it will prevent his being exposed in some way. People with low self-esteem do not like to admit they lie and often feel remorseful after they do; however, at the time of the incident that prompted the lie, they are so fearful of being exposed that they choose to lie as a way out.

Example:

Jill is embarrassed that she has no weekend plans, no date. When a coworker asks what she will be doing on the weekend, Jill lies and describes several fictitious outings to give the impression she has an active social life. Jill feels her lack of a full life is symbolic of her inadequacy.

Example:

Trying desperately to fit in at her new sales clerking job, Heidi lies and says her new budget-store outfit came from an expensive boutique. She feels incompetent knowing she has mishandled her money in the past and that her present job barely covers all her living expenses and credit card bills.

Example:

Jackson stays home from work on Tuesday, calling in to say he is sick. In actuality, he is depressed as the result of an incident at work the day before. In front of several coworkers, his colleague, Jerry, had told a joke that included Jackson's behavior at a recent meeting, teasing him. Jerry had not meant it in a derogatory way and no one had taken it as such; Jackson, however, was deeply insulted and embarrassed.

As a result of perceived frequent criticism, often when none is intended, those with LSE also practice observing others: they become "watchers." They watch what others do and how they do it, and then try to emulate what they see, striving diligently to "do it right." While watching, they remain anxious that they will be called upon to respond to a question they can't answer or asked to participate in something they don't know how to do; they fear they may overlook something important and still not get it "just right." As a result, they often become obsessive and perfectionistic.

JANE: life with John

When Jane had begun worrying that John might not love her, she decided she must try harder to please him. One evening she fixed his favorite food for dinner and, as was her habit, began visualizing how the evening would go, including the exact words she hoped John would say. She envisioned him coming in the door eagerly seeking her out because he had missed her as much as she had him. She pictured his eyes lighting up when he discovered the meal she had prepared and imagined his words of praise and affection. She envisioned them laughing and talking through dinner, lingering over dessert and coffee, followed by a romantic encounter.

Thirty minutes before John was to arrive home, Jane showered, combed her hair, and put on new clothes. She placed fresh flowers in the crystal vase, a wedding present given by the friends who had introduced them. She wanted everything to be perfect.

Jane expected John to be home by 6:15 each evening since his work day technically ended at 6:00. On this particular day when he was a few minutes late, Jane grew more anxious and started watching out the window. The CD she had put on ended. She wanted a particular song to be playing when John came through the front door, thinking he would immediately recognize its significance. She started the tape over and did so twice more before she saw his headlights pulling into the driveway. She vowed to herself not to ask him why he was late.

When John entered the house, Jane was waiting in the foyer. John, who was tired as well as nervous about the time, gave her a kiss, secretly wishing she wouldn't always be standing there when he came into the house. Jane didn't move and John had to step sideways to pass her in the small entrance way. He turned down the hall to take his briefcase into his study.

Having anticipated a more lengthy reunion, Jane felt waves of disappointment wash over her. Following him into the bedroom, she told him how much she had missed him that day. John felt trapped as Jane stood in the doorway and gently moved her to one side, saying, "Do I have time for a quick shower?" "Sure," she had responded, in a voice barely audible. After she had spent the whole day fixing this special dinner and preparing for the "perfect" evening, he hadn't even noticed the music she had so ceremoniously selected or commented on the table setting. She wondered then why she continued doing so much for him when he was so unappreciative. Angrily, she turned off the CD player.

Jane's emotions spiraled downward; she felt deeply hurt. She had just dished up dinner when John joined her at the table. He remarked that the table certainly looked attractive and the food looked and smelled great! Jane remained silent and took note that he hadn't mentioned the vase.

When Jane reached over to pour some wine for John, he said "I'd better not. I have some work to finish after dinner." Jane felt her heart in her throat. She felt humiliated! How dare he devote the evening to work after all she had done? Jane spent the remainder of the meal berating John in her head—going over and over his acts of insensitivity and neglect.

They ate in silence, with John trying to initiate conversation and Jane avoiding eye contact. Her head filled with

*self-recrimination. Did she really think that John looked for-
ward to coming home to her from his posh office? She wished
she had not put candles on the table, surmising that this, too,
had been a foolish gesture. She wished she could get up and
blow them out but felt she did not have the strength to rise
from her chair. She kept reminding herself of how "stupid" she
was.*

*John asked Jane if she was feeling all right. "Just tired,"
she responded. Indeed, she felt so exhausted that eating was a
chore. To cover what she was feeling, she asked John a few
questions. She didn't want him probing more about how she
was acting, since she had so obviously made a fool of herself.*

*By this time, Jane was so depressed she could barely con-
centrate on what John was saying. Inside, she just wished she
could disappear. She could hardly wait to get out of the room—
and away from him. He hadn't even noticed her new clothes.*

Jane had thought John would love her more if she did things
"right" and tried hard to set up the perfect dinner. She had attended to each minute detail: she had fixed the perfect meal, put wine
in the ice bucket, placed flowers on the table in a special vase,
selected the perfect song to be playing, dressed in new clothes,
and had everything timed precisely for his arrival. In seeing and
believing imperfection to be synonymous with inadequacy, Jane
placed enormous pressure on herself. She thought that her perfection would produce specific desired results; when it did not, she
felt humiliated and angry.

People with low self-esteem also often refuse to perform what
appear to be ordinary, simple tasks because they fear that something might go wrong or that they might not be able to perform
adequately.

JANE: parallel parking

When Jane eventually started back to work after her divorce, she would occasionally go out to a movie or dinner with two women from work. When it was her turn to drive, she would become extremely anxious, fearing that she might have to parallel park or that she might not be able to find the restaurant easily. Jane always had difficulty parallel parking and pictured herself trying unsuccessfully to get into the parking space. She knew she would be embarrassed when the other women saw her struggling to do something so simple. She became more anxious as the time drew near to perform this task, one that she believed was easy for everyone else.

On one of these occasions, Jane made excuses by saying that her car was running poorly and she hadn't had time to get it to a garage. On the second evening she was to be the driver, she called to say she was sick and encouraged her friends to go on without her.

Jane feels too uncertain about her driving skills to trust that she can complete the task without looking incompetent. She is fearful and anxious about appearing deficient at something she believes others do with ease. She is not aware that many people have difficulty parallel parking because it is a subject she would never bring up. She is also not aware that she could tell her friends that she doesn't "do" parallel parking. Instead she makes excuses as to why she cannot drive. Her friends, unaware of all this, may perceive her as uncooperative, selfish, and rigid, or they may become annoyed with her excuses and begin to wonder what is really going on. Their private conclusions about Jane's motives may be far more negative than the reality.

Jane feels that she is not as skilled as others but is too anxious to do anything that might correct her deficiencies. Instead of practicing parallel parking, she avoids any situation where she might be called on to do it. Through her avoidance of the task, she distances herself from the immediate anxiety but does nothing to alter or correct her perceived deficiency.

This pattern of avoidance is a serious problem for those with low self-esteem. They practice withdrawing from the threatening situation and are unable to reduce or eliminate the fear, in this case, that of learning to parallel park. Jane could find a friend to help her master this skill or even go to a driving school if she did not want to confide in someone she knows. This would be a healthy response to recognizing that her skill level needs to be increased. Most people with LSE, however, do not do this; instead, they continue to avoid any new demand that causes them distress rather than finding a way to overcome it.

The need to be constantly vigilant is exhausting for those with LSE as they attempt to "size up" each new situation, assess what is expected, and determine what their response will be. However, as we will discuss later, these assessments may not be accurate, further complicating the world for those with low self-esteem.

• *A note of comparison with those with healthy self-esteem:*

People with healthy self-esteem do not think they are less adequate in general than others and, therefore, do not incessantly worry about how they will perform. Instead, they perceive themselves as dealing with most situations appropriately and adequately. They do not carry with them the fear that something frightening or negative is about to happen. They are not afraid that they are about to do something that will be outrageous; instead, they have confidence that they will meet the demands of any situations they encounter.

Additionally, those with healthy self-esteem are able to admit the extent of their skills and are able to laugh about a situation, such as finding it difficult to parallel park. Because they openly discuss such experiences with others, they are aware that many people have difficulty learning to parallel park or to do other similar tasks; therefore, they do not view needing assistance to learn such a skill as a blemish on their character or a sign of inadequacy.

2.   Fear of revealing one's inadequacies to others, which could result in disapproval, criticism, rejection, or blame.

A common fear of those with LSE is that others who see their inadequacies, observe their mistakes, or witness them doing something "inappropriate," will judge them. They feel they must be very careful not to make a mistake because they fear others will laugh at them or ridicule them. They, therefore, are vigilant in observing themselves and others in a continuing effort to do what is acceptable, believing that a mistake will result in the criticism or disapproval they so desire to avoid.

As a result, they become anxious in any situation where they do not know what is expected. They tend to be nervous when performing in front of others, when doing any new task they have not totally mastered, or when interacting in social settings where they are unaware of the rules. They will surmise that others know things they do not, that others are more articulate and skilled in day-to-day living, that others know what is "appropriate" and expected. Their low self-esteem causes them to be anxious and fearful about making a mistake that others will recognize.

Contrary to what one might think, low self-esteem and success are not incompatible. Many people who have extremely low self-esteem are achieving at high levels in their careers. (More details on achievement are presented later in this chapter.)

Example:

> *Shaun is a highly successful stock analyst. Though he has been at his present job for eight years, he cannot relax. While he knows he excels at his work, he also recognizes he does not relate well with people—they often seem offended by the things he says. Consequently he takes his breaks alone and always leaves the building at lunchtime to avoid interaction with coworkers. When asked questions unrelated to his work, he answers briefly and avoids offering personal information or opinions, fearing others will be critical of what he has to say or how he lives his life. When asked anything in the area of expertise where he is secure, he goes to the other extreme, commenting at great length, clarifying and explaining in detail, often sounding pompous and arrogant.*

When we see someone like Shaun, who appears to be overly confident, even self-centered, yet who purposely avoids social interaction, we often label him as stuck-up or conceited. We would not easily recognize that he has LSE. In fact, those with LSE regularly overcompensate in areas of their lives where they do feel confident and competent, attempting to convince themselves and others of their adequacy. At the same time, they avoid those areas where they know they are unskilled. Inside, they are insecure, thinking that others do not like them, knowing they don't fit in. Attempting to win respect while needing approval and attention, they may brag and flaunt their areas of expertise. When these efforts to get recognition and admiration fail, they may retaliate with criticism and sarcasm or act as though they don't care; they may try to cover their feelings of rejection with either an air of superiority or one of disinterest while feeling the world is ominous and even terrifying. (More details about superiority-inferiority in Chapter 6.)

Years of past emotional deprivation and neglect may explain why people with low self-esteem find the world unpredictable, threatening, and confusing. They may not recognize, however, that they bear the scars of a background that thrived on disapproval and emotional abuse because they have nothing else with which to compare it. Now, like visitors in a foreign land, they frequently find they do not know what is expected of them. They remember being strongly criticized at times when they had no inkling of having done anything wrong or even out of the ordinary. They are reminded of the countless situations in life when they were unaware of how to respond or behave. They remember being reprimanded and berated for simple mistakes. They recall the chuckles, smirks, and rolled eyes they noticed when they shared their opinions or ideas. These real or imagined happenings all combine to create extreme anxiety, so they fear making another "blunder" that others will see and label as strange.

Further confounding the situation is the fact that acceptable and customary behavior varies within cultures and within subgroups; there is no consistent standard to follow. This adds to the confusion as the person with LSE tries to determine what is "right." The fact that his perceptions may be faulty can lead to inaccurate summations and ultimately inappropriate behaviors that don't "fit" this particular setting.

Example:

Leo works in an all-male environment, one where telling sexually suggestive jokes is encouraged and where those who do so are applauded. In another social environment and in an attempt to "fit in," he repeats these jokes and finds, to his dismay, that this audience is not only unresponsive but actually offended by his remarks.

Most likely Leo has come from a dysfunctional home in which the rules were different in some ways from those of the surrounding culture. Consequently, he does not know what is "normal" or "healthy" behavior in many areas of his life, for he only knows what he was taught, what he observed, or what he has learned through experiences inside of a dysfunctional setting. He does not know how to discriminate when and under what circumstances a behavior is acceptable, and when and under what circumstances it is not.

Does my personal history provide a reliable guide for navigating the interpersonal world? How will I know what is socially acceptable? How will I know what to do or not to do in a new situation? The following demonstrates the dilemma:

- *I think I know, but I don't.* I may think that something I have learned is normal when it isn't.

- *I think I know and I do.* I do know some things that are normal to others.

- *I know I don't know, but I don't know what I don't know.* I may be aware that there are likely accepted rules that others know, but I am unsure what they are. This is especially true in any new situation.

- *I don't know; I think others know, but they don't know either.* If I am in another dysfunctional system, I don't not know the rules, but I try to acquire them, unaware that these rules are also dysfunctional.

When customs and behaviors have been modeled and taught to us as a way of life, our only means of judging what is unacceptable is through our personal filtering system—our own perceptions and interpretation of those perceptions. These views, of course, were constructed and molded by that same dysfunctional environment that produced our low self-esteem; thus, we have nothing different to compare it with and no way to sort out the generally acceptable from the unacceptable. Until we learn the deficiencies or inaccuracies of that environment from some other source, our system remains skewed.

In essence, we repeat what we have been taught until we learn a new set of skills to replace the old ones. Even if we recognize that a specific set of behaviors was wrong or destructive, we continue to use those old methods to cope with life's challenges because we feel competent performing the behaviors we have practiced the most. Simply saying "I will never discipline like my parents did" or "I will never drink like my father did" does not guarantee that we will act differently. Unless we actually learn new ways to deal with the frustration and pressures of life and practice these to the point of proficiency, we will behave in the same way our parents did. *The desire to do differently is insufficient in itself; it must be accompanied by the acquisition of new skills or we will become like the parent we swore we would never imitate.* This is one reason why people who were beaten as children may in fact beat their own kids, even though they have determined to be different.

Another reason why we stay stuck in old patterns is that over time, we become tolerant of inappropriate behavior. People who have generally been mistreated become accustomed to it. They are much more likely to react to abusive behavior as normal than are people who have been respected and well cared for. For example, an adult child of an alcoholic parent may vow to never become involved with an alcoholic. Unfortunately, he may be so comfortable with the behaviors that accompany alcoholism that he fails to recognize them for what they are; he has no basis for comparison, no experience with normal partnering behavior. Without this insight, he mistakenly assumes these dysfunctional patterns of relating are normal and then gets involved with an alcoholic because he does not recognize the signs.

We do what we know, and we cannot do what we do not know. We must become aware of what we do not know and then seek a way to acquire the information and skills we are lacking.

The main way a person with LSE tries "to know" or to add to his repertoire is by watching others. He could ask questions about what he doesn't know, but he is afraid to approach others to get help in "knowing" because he feels that asking others would mean revealing the depth of his ignorance and giving others reason to think there is something wrong with him. To avoid demonstrating his perceived inadequacy, he determines that he must figure out the answers for himself. Realizing his appraisals may not be accurate, his data may not be complete, he worries about what he has overlooked or what he has learned that is inaccurate in other settings. The person who "doesn't know" could also take classes or research the issue to get the information needed. Whether or not he makes an effort to garner the information he needs will depend on whether he is a "Floater" or a "Paddler" as explained later in this chapter.

Observing others in order to determine what is appropriate can be problematic for another reason. By following what others do, the person may adopt behaviors that do not agree with his own standards or values. Because he doubts his judgment, he discounts his objections. Also, his desire to be accepted may be so great that he will compromise his standards.

Example:

Starting a new job after graduating from college, Belle continues to attend parties given by her coworkers even though she is uncomfortable with the drinking, inappropriate sexual behavior, and drugs that are present. She is afraid to turn down these invitations for fear others will not like her and will treat her differently at work.

Example:

Jamie, who is new at his job, joins his fellow workers in gossiping, ridiculing, and ignoring another worker in order to be accepted by the group.

The person with LSE seems unaware that others frequently ask questions, readily admitting that at times they need information. Instead, he sees his problem of "not knowing" as unique and a sign of some major deficit. In so doing, he denies himself access to information that others receive regularly.

For example, the person with LSE may find himself in a situation where a discussion takes place about a subject on which he is uninformed. Others are chiming in with their opinions, and he wants to participate but doesn't know what to say. The fact that nearly everyone else has spoken suggests to him that this is a topic he should be well-versed in or at least conscious of. He becomes very embarrassed because he doesn't have an opinion. Rather than say that he is unfamiliar with the issue, which he thinks might reveal some inadequacy about him, he remains quiet and self-conscious; he may even make an excuse to escape, going to the bathroom, remembering a call he needs to make, or suddenly looking at his watch and stating that he is late for an appointment.

The person with low self-esteem imagines that others are much more focused on his behavior than is the case. In his watchful quest to acquire information so that he will appear "normal," he becomes self-focused and believes that others are as aware of him and his behaviors as he is himself; he erroneously views himself as central to the universe, imagining that the moods and actions of others are a reaction to him. In truth, others are probably not that cognizant of his behavior; they may not be attending to him closely and may not be able to discern anything unusual. In fact, they may not have any reaction to his behavior at all.

Example:

When his supervisor first approaches him each morning, Nate watches closely to determine her mood. When she seems withdrawn, quiet, or irritated, Nate immediately assumes that he has done something wrong. In truth, she is going through a tumultuous divorce and her moods have nothing to do with Nate.

The past is a powerful teacher and the person with low self-esteem may have experienced the cruelty of others in the form of hostile teasing, ridicule, unjust assumptions, and criticism. She learns to expect similar treatment in the present and to anticipate what will trigger these reactions from others. Even as a child, she realized that many people react with hostility to any behavior that is different from what they want or expect. Now, as an adult, she still fears becoming the target of resentment and tries to blend in with the crowd. At the same time, she is reminded once again that she doesn't know all she needs to know to fit in, and more importantly, doesn't even know what crucial pieces of the puzzle are missing.

JANE: dealing with a new experience

Early in their courtship, John asked Jane to have dinner with him at an elegant restaurant. Jane, who had grown up in a poor home, had never eaten in such an expensive place. She was very pleased that John wanted to take her there but immediately became anxious that she might not know how to act. She considered making an excuse but realized that if she wanted their relationship to continue, she would have to face such situations. At the same time, she didn't feel comfortable sharing her reluctance with John. She thought that his view of her would be negatively affected if he recognized how inexperi-enced she was and how inadequate she felt. She decided that she would just follow John's lead at the dinner, figuring that if she watched him closely, she would be able to act appropriate-ly. She continued, however, to be very anxious.

The evening of the dinner, all seemed to be going well. When they were seated in the restaurant, the waiter approached and handed them each a menu. John told her to pick out any-thing she wanted because this was a special evening marking their two-month anniversary. Jane grinned at John, very pleased with his attentiveness. Looking at the menu, however, her heart sank and her pulse accelerated as she realized she didn't under-stand the list of foods before her and certainly didn't know how to pronounce them. She felt foolish and embarrassed. John would soon see how dumb she really was.

Then she remembered her plan and said to John. "Since you've been here before, John, what would you recommend?" John, who seemed pleased that she had asked his opinion, described one of the entrees he had eaten before and Jane quickly replied, "Great, I'll try that," feeling like she had just dodged another bullet.

Jane's fear and anxiety at being in an unknown situation are obvious. To cope with her anxiety and fear, she decided to "walk through it," devising a plan to watch John in order to determine what the appropriate actions were. She tried to anticipate the pos-sible pitfalls but was momentarily panicked when she saw the menu. She recovered, however, and returned to her plan to ask John to recommend something. By agreeing with his suggestion, she didn't risk making a mistake in her choice or in her pronunci-ation of the entrée. This was actually a clever way to deal with her uncertainty, but Jane will probably not look back on this event with an appreciation for her resourcefulness. Instead, she will focus on her ignorance and feel diminished. Unfortunately, Jane did not realize that she could simply have told John the truth. Most likely, he would not have been critical of Jane's inexperience but instead he might have been pleased that he was treating her to something new.

- *A note of comparison with those with healthy self-esteem:*

People with healthy self-esteem do not automatically anticipate that they will receive disapproval, rejection, criticism, or blame. Plus if they do receive it, they are less likely to personalize it; rather they more often view the criticism of their work as constructive, the rejection of their invitation as normal for people who have busy lives, or the disagreement with their suggestion as information to consider. If they feel they have been blamed unfairly, they know they have the option to assert themselves and confront the issue in a reasonable manner. They are more likely to be able to assess rationally whether the responses have merit and then decide how to deal with the situation. They are not constantly on the defensive as is the person with low self-esteem.

People with healthy self-esteem feel that if a situation arises, they can admit to their lack of knowledge and ask for assistance without feeling embarrassed or inadequate. They have confidence that they can, in some way, meet the challenges that arise.

THINGS TO REMEMBER

- Everyone makes mistakes. Making a mistake does not mean you are inadequate or incompetent.

- Everyone does and says things they later regret.

- Everyone has embarrassing moments.

- Others are not as aware of what you say or do as you are. They are usually focused on their own concerns.

- Being likable does not mean that everyone will like you.

- Everyone experiences rejection, whether in job interviews, possible romantic relationships, or simply by insensitive people.

- Everyone experiences disapproval. You can't please everyone all the time.

- Being imperfect is not synonymous with being inadequate. No one is perfect!

- Others will only respect you to to the degree that you demonstrate respect for yourself.

Note: Jane and John's relationship does not rise to the level of true intimacy. Jane is fearful of revealing her true self to John, thinking he will not want to continue the relationship if he sees who she really is: how she thinks and how fearful she is. This may or may not be true, but a relationship is doomed if the people involved do not feel free to be themselves. If John really loves Jane and comes to understand her struggles, she can be more free to work on them openly, giving John the opportunity to support her.

If John becomes aware of Jane's problem but chooses to end the relationship without allowing her time to work through her issues, his actions will say something about the level of his commitment. Because Jane fears losing him, she is reluctant to find out how John may choose to respond.

3. Fear of losing what one has; fear that success cannot be sustained; fear of abandonment.

People with LSE are not only afraid that they will not succeed, they question whether they can keep what they have managed to attain. Lacking confidence in themselves, they may question whether they can maintain their present level of productivity. They fear that people will think less of them as they reveal themselves. They constantly fear losing things that are precious to them, including relationships, career, and future security.

Example:

Carla is a successful psychologist who has developed a thriving practice in just two years. With an excellent referral base, she receives calls from more prospective clients than she can fit into her schedule. Her practice is doing better than she ever imagined. Having difficulty believing that her efforts are paying off and that her dreams may be coming true, she begins to worry about what might go wrong that would destroy it. She becomes obsessed with the fear of losing the status and success she has achieved and develops a sleep disorder.

Those who suffer from low self-esteem have experienced many losses in their lives, including lost opportunities, loss of dignity, failed relationships, and the loss of a true sense of self. Fear and anxiety have contributed to their inability to take advantage of opportunities, rendering them unable to realize their full potential. Blocking the attainment of dreams, these emotions have also paralyzed creativity (these individuals avoid trying new things for fear they will fail or look foolish). In addition, they have inhibited ambition (they feel defeated and exhausted) and stifled motivation (they expect to lose). These losses have taken their emotional toll on such people, leaving a lingering sadness; like foam on the top of a glass of beer, it slowly dissipates, only to reappear when more is poured.

With past and future dreams set aside, people with LSE may feel too discouraged, too fearful, too depleted of energy to risk doing anything different from the way they have done it in the past. As a result, they may choose safety over challenges, self-preservation over growth.

As a result of these many losses, the future may look bleak, with only more disappointment ahead. Labeling themselves "failures," those with low self-esteem lower their expectations of themselves even more as they resign themselves to a life of thwarted goals. In so doing, they may become underachievers, accomplishing far less than their abilities or intelligence warrant. With this loss of self-confidence, over time they develop a fatalistic view of life.

Those with LSE worry that when their present partner recognizes their deficiencies, their relationship will be over. Those with LSE tend to think that they have somehow fooled the other person into thinking they are fully healthy adults; now they fear that their loved one will see the truth of their inadequacies and will not want to continue in the relationship. Some individuals with LSE respond to this fear as Jane did, becoming controlling, trying to limit their partner's contacts with the outside world. Others indulge their partners, becoming submissive and subservient;

still others shower their partners with attention and expensive gifts, attempting to impress the loved one and convince the partner of what a great asset they are. When a loved one has complaints about the behavior of her LSE partner, the partner may jump to the conclusion that the end is in sight because LSE sufferers tend to magnify most complaints so that they mean much more than is intended. In other words, the person cannot focus on the one specific issue that has been brought up but instead blows it out of proportion because he cannot bear to hear criticism.

As Jane fixed dinner for John, she feared losing him. She constantly questioned his feelings for her. She saw his interest in being with his friends as "not wanting to be with her." When he didn't arrive home at the time she thought he should, she read this as his not being excited to see her, an indication that he didn't care about her.

Throughout their relationship, Jane continued to be amazed that John had chosen her to be his life partner. Her feeling of inferiority contributed to her need to please him and to know that he valued her. When this attempt to prove herself seemed not to reap the expected rewards, she tried out of desperation to control him. She acted as if given the chance, John would try to get away from her. She feared that if he spent time with others, he would prefer them to her and ultimately reject her. She went to extremes to give the impression that they had the perfect life, totally devoted to each other and untouched by the outside world. John became annoyed and confused by Jane's behavior, especially her need to control him. At first he worked hard to please her, thinking she was adjusting to being married; later he merely tried to appease her so she wouldn't become depressed.

As with Jane, when we truly doubt our ability to sustain success, our anxiety is greatly increased and our performance is greatly affected, causing us to sabotage that success and seemingly prove that our fears were justified. Thus success itself becomes a source of anxiety; we cannot enjoy it if we are waiting for it to disappear. We may even wish that it had not happened, that we had not gotten the promotion, for example, fearing that we will not be able to live up to the increased expectations and will ultimately fail, causing more humiliation than if we had not received the promotion in the first place.

Example:

Terri, a sophomore in college, has achieved excellent grades as well as praise from her instructors. She tells herself, however, that she has just been lucky so far, that she has taken easy classes. She fears the new term, when her classes will surely reveal how really unintelligent she is.

Thus, those with LSE desire to be successful, but success has components that also create fear, for they anticipate that success raises the expectations of others. They surmise that others will expect them to have increased knowledge, improved skills, and due to their past good grades, continued success—success that LSE sufferers doubt can be sustained.

Example:

Tyler attended trade school to become a mechanic. He has been excitedly looking for a job for several weeks and receives a phone call saying he has been hired. At first he is elated and calls several friends to tell them the good news. Then he begins to worry about what his new employers will expect from him. Will he be able to do whatever is required? Was his training really adequate? What if they don't think he's good enough? By the end of the day, Tyler is frantic.

In this case, Tyler does what is typical of LSE sufferers: he anticipates the possible "negative" outcomes until he becomes convinced that they are true predictions of the future, rather than speculation. He becomes frantic because he believes that he has made himself vulnerable and that he is destined to fail.

Example:

> *Mary is 46 and recently divorced; she is returning to the work force after 21 years. After training, she begins working as a reporter's assistant for a large newspaper. When she receives a major promotion two years later, she becomes terrified, wondering if she can handle the increased responsibilities. Very proud of his daughter, her father tells her she is on her way up the ladder: it will now be only a matter of time before she rises to the top of the company. Uncomfortable with his growing expectations and fearful of disappointing him, Mary becomes anxious and agitated, and she begins to regret receiving the promotion.*

- *A note of comparison with those with healthy self-esteem:*

People with healthy self-esteem do not irrationally worry about losing what they have achieved or now possess. They believe they are worthy of what they have, including relationships, career success, economic and social standing, and material possessions.

They do not fear that they will make some fatal mistake that will cause their lives to come crumbling down around them but are confident that the personal resources they possess will continue to be effective in dealing with life.

People with healthy self-esteem can enjoy and celebrate their successes. They believe their rewards have been earned, they are confident in their ability to continue to meet challenges, and they are free to accept rewards and praise. They do not fear prosperity but believe they deserve it and expect it to continue.

While they may have suffered losses in the past, they believe in their ability to handle unforeseen loss should it occur. They do not anticipate future losses to be extraordinary but rather those that people routinely handle.

Two Extremes: Underachievers and Overachievers

People with LSE generally find themselves at one of the extremes of achievement, either as an overachiever or as an underachiever. Some take the road of continually channeling their energies into attempts to receive recognition, approval, and affirmation, becoming highly successful in their careers and educational endeavors; they are driven; they are "overachievers." They may become workaholics in their attempts to increase their sense of self-worth: obsessive about completing projects, constantly striving for perfection, or continually taking on huge new undertakings. They may spend endless hours glued to their work—all this effort spent to receive the sought-after recognition that will prove their self-worth while neglecting other parts of their lives.

Winning awards, earning degrees and promotions, and receiving praise does help the person feel better about herself for a while. When this feeling of well-being wears off, however, the need for positive attention is still there, requiring more effort and more demonstrations of praise and respect. In this way, the person tries to heal an internal wound through external performance. Like putting a bandage or salve on a deep cut, it doesn't work; it only provides temporary relief.

Others slink back in fear, never realizing their skills or talents. In their insecurity, they are afraid to try new things and are frightened by the challenges they face, vulnerable to the possibility of failure and humiliation. While these people are often capable and bright, they do not recognize or utilize their skills because their motivation has been so repressed and their fear of failure is so great. They have become "underachievers," individuals who are achieving far less than they are capable of.

Figure 1: Two Extremes: Achievement

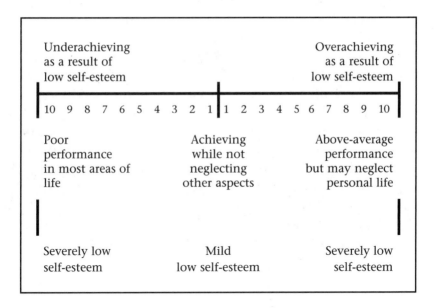

The diagram above illustrates the degrees of dysfunction of overachieving and underachieving and how those with LSE usually fall at either end of the spectrum of achievement. The high numbers at each end indicate individuals with more severe conditions of low self-esteem, while the lower numbers indicate those

with a less severe experience. Thus, the more a person is ham-
pered by low self-esteem, the more likely he is to react by underachieving or overachieving.

4. *Fear of re-experiencing humiliation, depression, devastation, or*
   despair.

When criticism, rejection, or disapproval comes, or when the
person with LSE behaves in some way that she deems "wrong,"
the result is often an immediate spiraling down into humiliation,
depression, devastation, or despair. She feels immense pain, possibly over a prolonged period of time. In severe cases, this stage may
be so traumatic that she considers suicide.

Fearing that these strong and terrifying emotions will return
along with the hopelessness that accompanies them, the individual experiences extreme anxiety. She is, quite understand-
ably, apprehensive of any situation that might resemble a past
one that triggered these emotions. She avoids people, places, or
activities that she associates with these negative feelings. She
becomes hyper-vigilant, like a person who has been bitten by a
dog and watches closely to see that no dogs lurk nearby. Thus,
extremely emotional experiences become a source of fear and anxiety in themselves; because they are so painful, the person remains
anxious afterwards, fearing their return and acting in ways to avoid
that possibility.

Example:

Kennedy recently attended a dinner party given by her new
neighbors. Following the meal, everyone was asked to gather
around the dining room table for a game of Trivial Pursuit.
Kennedy, who is very self-conscious and hates table games,

*could not think of a gracious way to decline and was assigned
to a team. Throughout the game, she was seldom able to contribute. She was so anxious that she couldn't concentrate; she
was sure everyone was thinking she wasn't very bright. As the
game continued, she began to feel more and more humiliated
and, continuing to berate herself, talked herself into depressive
state. As soon as she could get the courage to do so, she excused
herself, saying she needed to get home. Later she vowed to
never again play table games because she was not competent
at them and would only end up feeling humiliated and
depressed again.*

- *A note of comparison with those with healthy self-esteem:*

People with healthy self-esteem have experienced embarrassment, but usually only infrequently and never to a very intense
degree. They are confident, and with that confidence comes a
belief that they are basically worthwhile, so that making a mistake
is not an indication of some deficit within them. In addition, they
may never have felt humiliation, devastation, or despair.
Consequently, they have no fear that these emotions will "strike"
unexpectedly.

When issues arise, people with healthy self-esteem are generally able to handle them in a constructive manner, so they are
unfamiliar with this level of pain and anxiety. They believe they
are able to deal with normal tragedies that may come their way,
but they do not anticipate them nor worry about them without
sufficient reason.

Example:

Martha has a PhD and works as a scientist. She is very bright and skilled, but due to her low self-esteem, she devalues her education and skills and views herself as less competent than her fellow workers. Fearful of looking foolish and because of these feelings of inadequacy, she seldom speaks up in meetings or shares her opinions with fellow workers. Every meeting is agonizing and afterwards, Martha feels devastated. She considers giving up her lucrative and prestigious job because she cannot face the thought of suffering more emotional turmoil.

It is important to point out at this juncture that Martha is indeed competent. Her problems are not caused by a lack of skills or an inability to understand complex problems or goals; instead, Martha's problem is solely what she says to herself. Once she begins berating herself, she cannot stop the pattern of negative thinking. As it continues, she suffers from periods of severe depression. Then because she dreads doing anything that might cause these feelings of devastation and depression to return, she is unable to do anything different. She is caught in a web of self-destructive thinking and the behaviors that accompany this type thinking. Low self-esteem is negatively controlling her life.

Attaining New Skills: Floaters and Paddlers

While fear and anxiety have the power to control lives and obstruct growth, they are obstacles that can be hurdled. Many with LSE, however, tend to stay stuck, as though encased in cement. They face the same disappointments repeatedly without considering doing anything about them (staying in a job with low pay or no benefits, for example, or remaining in an abusive relationship). They seem to accept life as it comes without recognizing that they could do something differently, that they could take the wheel and drive their life in another direction (take classes, learn new skills, develop new interests, go to therapy). These people are Floaters. Atop their life rafts, they simply float, taking the waves of life as they come, rather than paddling to a destination of their choosing. They either do not know or do not believe that their efforts can make a difference. Unaware of the oars beside them, they hope that if a storm arises, someone will come to their rescue and pull them ashore; otherwise, they may never take the steps that would provide a stable foundation for building a fulfilling life. They believe that life is more difficult for them than for others; they do not see that others have worked and struggled to get where they are. In this way, they do not have to face their fears but keep them at bay.

Floaters tend to keep their emotions to themselves, and they think that others should do the same. They are usually fearful of displays of emotions, anxious about communication that is controversial, and uncomfortable with talk of feelings in general. They tend to avoid intimate discussions. When someone tries to bring up topics of a personal nature, they may become quiet and refuse to participate, they may become defensive, or they may attack the other person in order to end the discussion and relieve their discomfort.

Example:

Brandy's mother suffered from low self-esteem and was a floater. She was fearful of conflict and any show of emotion. Whenever Brandy would get upset, her mother was quick to say, "There's no need to get upset" or "Just calm down."

This angered Brandy who became confused about what she was doing that needed to be corrected. She heard her mother saying that she was just overreacting and that the reason she had given for being upset was of no importance.

Over time, Brandy kept her negative feelings in check and avoided sharing them with anyone. Eventually, she buried her feelings, even from herself. She was no longer able to tell what she felt; she was numb. She, too, became a floater and remained so until she got involved in a recovery program for LSE sufferers and began to realize what had happened.

Most floaters are uninvolved when it comes to issues of personal growth. They quietly accept their present circumstances without even questioning them or looking for other alternatives. They do not focus on improving themselves, i.e., attending to personal growth; instead, they busy themselves with the practical and mundane demands of daily life. In this way they stay at a surface level with the world and themselves, never delving into self-examination.

Paddlers, on the other hand, are more introspective, frequently reading books, talking to others about personal growth issues, taking classes and setting personal goals that they want to achieve. They are more in touch with themselves, consciously attempting to grow emotionally and develop themselves more fully. While they may not have found the help they need, they are more in touch with their problems and they strive diligently to improve their lives and to find a way out of the darkness of low self-esteem. Many have been to one or more therapists who, unfortunately, did not know how to treat low self-esteem. Still, paddlers keep looking, determined to find the answers that will lead them to a more satisfying life.

"Floaters" must decide to become "paddlers," people who take charge of their lives, people who do what is necessary, within reason, to set realistic goals and do what is necessary to reach them. Paddlers are not content to float through life taking what comes their way, succumbing to the circumstances that first shaped their journey. They recognize that to have experienced circumstances that damaged their self-esteem is most unfortunate but to allow those circumstances to ruin their lives is tragic and unacceptable.

As with the attainment of any new skill, however, the ability to become a "paddler" requires:

- That we be aware of the need for developing new ways to think and live. We must also recognize that change is possible. This recognition and awareness is the first and most important factor in growth and change.

- That we have the desire to change, to overcome those obstacles that prevent us from doing or getting what we want in life. People can be different from how they are presently, but they have to truly want that transformation to occur.

- That we be aware of how to do a task or how to do it differently. For example, if you are not aware that you are a poor communicator, you probably won't do anything to improve your way of relating to others. And if you don't know how to do it differently, your patterns of communicating will remain the same. If, on the other hand, you are aware that you haven't been successful in relationships, you might conclude that communication is the problem; then you will need to acquire information about how to communicate differently.

- That we develop a plan. When people with healthy self-esteem decide that change is in order, they do something; they make a plan. If they decide they need new information or skills, they:

  1. ask others for the information to get started

  2. research it on the Internet

  3. read newspapers and magazines

  4. consult professionals

5. take classes

6. attend workshops

7. look for resource material at the library

• That we take steps toward becoming a Paddler by doing something today to achieve our goal. Tomorrow never comes; do something today. Take one step, no matter how small, towards accomplishing the task.

Interestingly, we can be Paddlers in our work lives and remain Floaters in our personal lives. Struggling with LSE, we may feel very insecure and uncertain how to proceed in our relationships or how to make other constructive personal decisions; we may have few friends and interests and continue floating because we don't know what or how to do things differently. At the same time we may feel confident at work where we understand the rules and expectations. As a result, we become paddlers in that environment, asserting ourselves in the development of our careers.

Unfortunately, many LSE sufferers who are Paddlers have not found the guidance they have sought to overcome their LSE. Due to the poor attitude toward—and lacking a real understanding of—low self-esteem, few therapists know how to treat LSE or how to guide those who suffer from it toward recovery. Instead, they basically ignore low self-esteem, labeling it merely as a symptom rather than the disorder it is. They treat the depression or the anxiety or focus on the relationship problems and never get to the core issue—low self-esteem. Thus, many people who suffer from LSE never get the help they need. (See *Low Self-Esteem Misunderstood & Misdiagnosed: Why You May Not Find the Help You Need*, Sorensen, Marilyn J., Wolf Publishing Co., 2002)

RECOVERY

People with LSE can overcome their fears by facing and walking through each fear as it arises. In most cases, as the person does so, they become aware that what seemed insurmountable is not really so but is actually possible. In this way, the person can gradually remove the fears that stand in their way and eventually eliminate fear as the controlling factor in their lives. Doing so, of course, is not an easy process but one well worth undertaking because fear forms roadblocks in life that greatly impede our journey. As we face each fear, we can begin to see the irrationality of those fears and we can then learn to respond to them in ways that are more constructive. With each fear we face in the process of our recovery, we break one link in the chain of low self-esteem.

THINGS TO DO

Exercise 1

People with LSE focus an inordinate amount of energy on their weaknesses and shortcomings. This excessive attention to their perceived deficiencies, of course, blocks their ability to feel good about themselves and to move forward toward their goals and dreams.

This exercise is intended to begin changing that negative focus— to get you to see your strengths and good qualities and ultimately to help you see yourself more favorably.

1. Make a list of your good qualities. (Are you caring, sincere, honest, fun? Are you kind, generous, patient, friendly, loyal, dependable? Are you a good listener? Are you thoughtful and do you do nice things for others? Do you let others know that you appreciate them? Can you be trusted? Can you be counted on to be there when someone is in need?) If you need help, consider what it is that you admire in others who you think of as "quality" people. If you have difficulty making this list, solicit help from a friend, family member, or your therapist.

2. Write these things on a 3 x 5 note card. Read this card 5 times a day, preferably aloud and preferably in front of a mirror.

3. Make a list of ways you've helped others. (Have you contributed to the poor, visited a sick friend or relative, done a favor for an elderly person in your neighborhood, helped dig someone's car out of a snowbank, taken food to someone just out of the hospital, helped someone fix a flat tire, given work to someone in need? Are you friendly to new coworkers? Do you give a call to friends or family when you know they are going through a hard time? Do you help out an elderly neighbor in any way?) Write these on one or more 3 x 5 note

cards, listing them as: "I am friendly to new coworkers" or "I help out my neighbors in any way I can" or "I donate time at the Humane Society" or whatever it is that you do. Then read your list 5 times a day for 60 days. Add any new things that come to mind.

4. How is your attitude? Make a list of the different behaviors or thoughts that are an indication of your attitude toward yourself and others. (Are you quick to step forward to help others in need? Do you treat others with respect? Are you demanding of others? Do you think of yourself as better or inferior to others? Do you think others are better or more knowledgeable than you? Are you overly self-focused? Are you rude or abrupt? Do you have a desire to share what you have with others less fortunate? Are you fearful much of the time? Do you do more for others than you should? Do you value the opinions of others more than your own?) These are important things to sort out in your own mind.

   Make separate cards that list the positive things you do and the negative things you do. Read each card daily, preferably at the beginning of each day. This will allow you to focus both on the behaviors that indicate a healthy attitude while also becoming more aware of the behaviors that indicate an attitude you would like to alter. Don't get down on yourself, however. We all need to do this exercise from time to time to be sure we are remaining balanced?

5. Continue reading your cards for at least 6 months.

How did you feel when you made this list? Was it hard to do? Did you need help? If so, can you see how negative you have been toward yourself? How did you feel when you read this list to yourself? Were you self-conscious? Were you able to recognize how you normally invalidate yourself? It's important to take stock from time to time in who we have become or are becoming as people. All to often we are swept along with life's responsibilities and don't take time to sit down and look at ourselves—both the positive and the negative—so that we can recognize and revel in how far we've come while also remaining conscious of how we can still improve. People with low self-esteem have difficulty looking at both sides at the same time, tending instead to primarily see the negative and then to become stuck. They have difficulty believing in their positive side or in recognizing that everyone has aspects of themselves that are good, but also those that could use improvement.

THINGS TO DO

Exercise 2

Realize that loss is difficult for everyone. If you have experienced abandonment and many losses in your life and you have low self-esteem, you will naturally fear future losses. It is nothing to be ashamed of; it is, however, important to recognize your fear and begin to face it. This exercise is a step in that direction.

1. Think about your past losses. Write them down, leaving space to write more information below each one.

2. Allow yourself to feel whatever emotions arise.

3. If possible, list the emotions you are feeling.

4. Think about these past losses you have recorded and ask yourself these questions. Were they the result of something you did or failed to do? If so, what? Underneath each loss you listed, write down what it was you did or failed to do that contributed to the loss.

5. Were any of these losses ones over which you had no control? Note this in your journal as well.

6. Taking one loss at a time, consider various options or alternative behaviors you might have implemented in place of those you used. For example, maybe you could have maintained a significant relationship if you hadn't been so controlling or if you had personally taken more responsibility for initiating time together. Write this down as well. If you can't come up with ideas, talk it over with a friend or your therapist. (Often we do not succeed because we expect a negative outcome. We then act in ways that produce those very results even though they are not the ones we wanted.)

7. Sit back in a comfortable chair, close your eyes, and imagine yourself back in the situation you consider a self-inflicted loss. But this time, insert in your recollection the behavior that could have replaced the original dysfunctional behavior. For example, if you now believe you should have initiated more contact, think of how you could have gone to the phone and called the person. In your mind, envision picking up the phone, dialing, and speaking to the person. Think of questions you might ask about the other person, such as about their work, health, family, pets, garden, etc. Think of specific information you might share from your own life, like movies you have seen, activities you have engaged in, new books you have read, or people you have seen. Repeat this visualization until you feel comfortable; then imagine yourself doing it differently in the future.

8. Do this with each of the losses you have suffered that you think you could have prevented.

How did it feel to do this exercise? Were you able to recognize how you might have helped engineer your own losses in the past? Were you able to identify ways you could have acted differently? Were you able to imagine yourself doing it differently the next time? KEEP PRACTICING.

THINGS TO DO

Exercise 3

Both overachieving and underachieving are undesirable because they imply an unhealthy response to one's fears. Both are ways to avoid dealing with our issues. This exercise is an attempt to invoke awareness of this problem.

1. Are you an overachiever or an underachiever? Write down the reasons for your answer.

2. If you are an underachiever, what skills or abilities do you think you possess that you have not utilized? Record these in your notebook.

3. If you are an overachiever, you have probably benefited in many ways. You may, however, have given up things in order to devote your efforts to accomplishing your goals. What have you given up? What have you avoided? Write these down.

4. Ask yourself if there is anything in particular you would like to do, learn, or experience? Think about this. Talk to others. Read about the particular subject. As you collect information about it, you may find it less threatening. As you get stronger, you may be able to make a plan and move in that direction.

How did you feel when you asked yourself these questions? Were you able to see how your fears have controlled your decisions and actions, how your fears have dictated the course of your life? In the future, try to assess your motivation before you act. Then try to direct your decisions towards bringing your overall goals to fruition.

THINGS TO DO

Exercise 4

When we develop ourselves personally, we grow and change; we are more interesting people because of these changes. When we do not set personal goals, we become stagnant and boring; we let life pass us by. This exercise is intended to stimulate your awareness, your introspection; it is intended to motivate you to become a paddler.

Think about the following:

1. Are you a Floater or a Paddler? Think about how you have lived your life to this point. Are you a go-getter or do you just wait for life to come to you? Do you have goals? Many floaters do not. Do you strive to improve who you are as a person or are you no more in touch with yourself, no more aware of who you are, than you were a year ago?

2. List the improvements, areas of awareness, or new skills you have added to your life in the last two years. If you cannot think of any, you are definitely a floater.

Goals can be placed in two categories, long-term and short-term. A long-term goal might include: deciding to take one class or workshop a year, deciding that you need to develop a better support system, or resolving to go to therapy.

A short-term goal is something you can accomplish in a relatively short period like a month or less. Short-term goals might include planning to call one person to initiate an activity, endeavoring to become a more grateful person by expressing appreciation to one person a week, or formulating a plan to choose a therapist.

3. Think of one short-term goal that you could set and accomplish in the next month. Reading a book on some self-help topic is an easy way to get started.

4. Take one step this week toward accomplishing this goal, e.g. visit your local library or bookstore and peruse the self-help section. Select a book and begin your journey.

When you have accomplished one new goal, ask yourself how you feel about your success? Would it be worthwhile to set more goals?

3

When Life is a Minefield

Jane: devastation & humiliation

One day Jane stopped at a deli to get a sandwich. She hated eating alone in public and so usually went to a drive-through or into a deli where she would purchase a sandwich and drink to take with her.

On this day, Jane entered the deli and walked to the counter. She did not see the man bending over the refrigerator, selecting a soda. After Jane had ordered, she also approached the cold drink machine, only then seeing and recognizing the man opening his soda can. He greeted her warmly and initiated conversation. Jane stiffened, responding halfheartedly to his greeting and question. As she did so, she watched his face, thinking she saw a smirk. She knew she was probably heavier than the last time he had seen her. Jane felt humiliation sweep over her. She was convinced that what she had detected was his disgust at her weight gain. She imagined him thinking that she was fat, "juicy gossip" that he would tell mutual acquaintances. She felt she was sinking into quicksand. She wanted to shrink away from him and looked for a way to escape.

Glancing at her watch, she feigned surprise and said, "Oh, no, I'm late for an appointment. Sorry, but I have to get going." She turned abruptly and fled from the deli, without retrieving or paying for the sandwich she had ordered. Quickly, she drove several blocks before pulling into a supermarket parking lot. There she parked in a remote corner and cried. She felt so foolish—why had she run out of the deli like that? Now she would never be able to go there again. Why was she so stupid, she wondered. Then her thoughts returned to the man in the store. What must he have thought? Within an hour he would be laughingly recounting their meeting; others would be laughing at her too. Jane returned home. For two days she felt depressed and despondent, unable to go out in public.

Those with LSE focus their energy and attention on trying to be "appropriate"—a word they use all too often to evaluate themselves. Thus, when a person with LSE does something he later thinks was wrong, inappropriate, or stupid, he experiences deep remorse, embarrassment, and humiliation. This occurs both when he has reached this conclusion himself and when he believes others have observed his blunder. If he also thinks that his error was significant, he slides further into devastation or even despair. Whether or not the incident was really important or whether the behavior was truly inappropriate does not matter. It is the perception and interpretation by the person with LSE that sets off the emotional reaction. In Jane's case she has a negative perception of herself and projects this on to others, like the man she encountered in the deli; she assumes he is reacting to her as disapprovingly as she is. Her emotions begin to take over and she then does something that later she views as inappropriate—runs out of the deli without her sandwich. This adds to her self-loathing and lack of self-respect.

The person with LSE experiences similar emotions whenever he feels criticized, ignored, put down, laughed at, or in any way devalued by others. Life becomes similar to walking through a minefield, never knowing when something will happen that will produce these extreme emotions. Examples in Jane's life like the one below have made Jane hypersensitive to negative responses from others.

JANE: a large woman

Jane is a large woman who has always been self-conscious about her size. When she was in junior high, she was already as tall as her teachers and much bigger than her classmates. Jane's mother, however, seemed totally oblivious to her feelings. She always wanted Jane to wear dresses even though Jane repeatedly told her she felt more comfortable in pants.

One winter when Jane was in college, her mother called to say that a group of friends and relatives were having a pre-Christmas dinner the day after Jane would arrive home. She told Jane the women had decided to wear long dresses and urged Jane to buy one. Disgusted and tired of this ongoing struggle, Jane reminded her mother that she felt like a hippo in a dress and would just wear pants (she didn't care if all the others were wearing long dresses but thought her mother could have spoken up on her behalf when it was first discussed). Jane's mother responded with "Oh, Jane, don't be that way." Jane felt diminished and angry, "Why do you keep harping on this? Don't you understand or care how I feel?" Sounding hurt, her mother changed the subject and soon they hung up. Jane felt deeply wounded. She wished she had somewhere else to go for the holidays.

Dreading the big dinner and more disapproval from her mother, Jane arrived home for vacation; she felt lethargic from depression.

Her mother told her she looked tired. The following morning, the day of the big dinner, Jane's mother handed Jane a wrapped package saying "I have an early Christmas present for you; open it now." Jane wondered what this was about but began removing the paper. She lifted out a red blouse and ankle-length skirt. She was dumbfounded and stared at her mother in disbelief. Her mother's face lit up as she said, "It's for you to wear tonight so you'll be dressed like all the rest of the women." Jane was speechless as she continued to stare at the clothing. She wanted to scream. She wanted to rip the clothing to shreds, but instead, she just sat there in silence. Jane's mother continued chattering, seeming not to notice that Jane was slumped in the chair, devastated.

That night Jane wore the new outfit to the dinner. She was quiet throughout the evening, only talking when asked a question. Inside, she was close to despair.

The Self-Esteem Attack

Most people with severe low self-esteem have experienced such situations which are actually self-esteem attacks–times when a person's low self-esteem is activated to the point where the person experiences extreme feelings of devastation and even despair. Consequently, they have also endured–and continue to endure–these attacks frequently throughout their lives without the ability to control them or even to stop the attacks in a timely fashion. Instead, they now try to avoid any situation that has the potential to go awry and end in a self-esteem attack. They work diligently trying to discern what to do, what not to do, and when or when not to do it because they dread the return of these feelings of devastation.

Those who have experienced self-esteem attacks describe them as tidal waves of despair washing over them unexpectedly and instantaneously. Some characterize an attack as falling into a deep dark hole or experiencing a dark cloud descending upon them. They talk about frequent experiences of terror and tell how they feel depressed, despairing, without hope; they talk about their thoughts of suicide.

When experiencing a self-esteem attack at its most debilitating level, individuals often become exhausted, remaining lethargic until the episode has passed. Some retreat to their beds in a near-fetal position and go into a deep, long-lasting sleep.

Others, when experiencing an attack, may distance themselves from their friends for varying periods of time, only venturing out when they have to go to work or to obtain necessities. They pull down the shades and hope no one will call. If friends do call, they do not answer the phone or else give a reason why they cannot talk. Later they make more excuses as to why they did not return the call.

The length and severity of these self-esteem attacks varies for individuals depending on several factors, including:

- The level or seriousness of the person's low self-esteem. (The lower the person's self esteem, the more severe the attack.)

- The amount of support the person has from other people. (The better the person's support system, the more likely she will recover sooner.)

- The amount of time that transpires between the occurrence of the Self-Esteem Attack and the receipt of support. (The less time the person spends in the devastation before receiving support, the more quickly the devastation can be defused.)

- The person's perspective on the situation that caused the Self-Esteem Attack. (The more extreme the person views the repercussions from the situation that caused the self-esteem attack, the more devastated she will be.)

- The level of the person's personal growth. (The more progress the person has previously made in working through these Self-Esteem Attacks, the less severe the devastation will be and the shorter the duration of these emotions.)

During periods of devastation following a self-esteem attack, some sob uncontrollably for long periods of time. They may abuse themselves with food, drugs, alcohol, or nicotine to relieve the pain. Throughout this self-esteem attack, they feel emotionally overwhelmed and possibly numb; their thoughts are not clear. In this state of devastation, the individual senses a serious threat to his ability to maintain emotional equilibrium. He may fear that he is losing control; he may express a wish to "die, vanish, melt into a puddle, or otherwise dissolve."

The devastation, humiliation, and despair that follow a self-esteem attack are all accompanied by a desperate and urgent desire to flee. The person frantically searches for a way to escape the situation, leave the room, get out of the car, or otherwise separate from those involved. Most often, however, she is unable to immediately escape from the situation because people and circumstances prohibit it. For instance, if she is at work, she may not be able to leave, though she may excuse herself and go to the restroom to get a few minutes' reprieve. If the person is sitting at a family dinner, attending a meeting, or out shopping with friends, she may realize that fleeing from the situation will only draw attention and curious speculation or even more negative reactions, the very responses she wants to avoid. In those circumstances, she will continue on with the event, striving to look and act normal. When possible, however, actually withdrawing from the event remains desirable—and is a path frequently taken.

In circumstances where the person with LSE feels both trapped and in a state of terror, she may visualize or emotionally experience her body retreating from the situation even though she has not moved. She does not hear what is going on; her mind assists her in departing from the trauma by shutting out her surroundings. When she is this upset, she does not want to be touched, especially by the person whom she perceives has provided the threat or hurt her, and she will physically pull away if the person reaches out to her.

A self-esteem attack can be so severe and the person so distraught that she actually becomes immobilized, unable to speak or move, although not all people with low self-esteem experience this. (Some also experience memory loss, discussed later in this chapter.) From a sense of physical heaviness or weakness, or from stark terror, the devastated person feels unable to rise from her chair or take a step. Inside, she is in turmoil, trying frantically to pull herself together before anyone notices. It may or may not be apparent to others that she is in this devastation stage; she may simply appear quiet and unresponsive.

All those who are experiencing a self-esteem attack realize that what they are *feeling* is abnormal; they wonder if others can tell what they are experiencing. If they perceive themselves as also *acting* strangely, they feel even more humiliated, dreading that those watching will label them as bizarre. This additional threat of further humiliation can accelerate the downward spiral of the self-esteem attack, making it even more severe and long lasting. And, if someone does comment on the behavior of the devastated person, these remarks only serve to exacerbate the situation.

Later when the extreme emotions that accompany a self-esteem attack have subsided, the individual feels deeply humiliated by her reaction. She may feel she can never return to the scene of the situation or face those who were present, imagining what they are now saying or thinking about her. She visualizes her family, friends, coworkers, acquaintances, anyone present, as analyzing, labeling, and laughing at her, though this is usually inaccurate

The duration of a self-esteem attack varies from situation to situation, from person to person. One may remain in this state for hours, days, or even weeks. Just as the time span and seriousness of the self-esteem attack varies, so does the frequency. A significant measure of growth in overcoming low self-esteem is seeing a decrease in the severity, the frequency, and the length of these bouts.

Triggering Incidents

The extreme emotions that accompany a self-esteem attack take place following one or a chain of events: a situation occurs and the person with LSE translates it internally as meaning something negative about herself; then, based on that analysis, she goes into a tailspin of depression, devastation, or possibly despair. The particular event that starts this process in motion is called the triggering incident or "trigger."

What to many people might seem an innocuous event or relatively small incident may be a trigger to the person with LSE. A situation that might not offend or that might go completely unnoticed by a person with healthy self-esteem may trigger the person with low self-esteem; a situation that might give only slight discomfort to the person with healthy self-esteem may seem a serious incident to someone with very low self-esteem. Why? Because it is not the incident itself that produces devastation, but the individual's interpretation of the incident and its relationship to that person's inner video. For the same reasons, what acts as a trigger to one person with low self-esteem may not trigger another who also deals with low self-esteem.

A relatively insignificant encounter to most people is a triggering incident to Jane. Coupled with her irrational conclusions, such an incident can set off a self-esteem attack. For example, Jane was already anxious about eating alone and went to the deli as a means of hiding. To then be "discovered" there by someone who knew her—the very thing she was attempting to avoid—was so disconcerting that Jane lost her composure. Jane doesn't adjust well to surprise situations; she became immediately aware of herself and projected onto the man the descriptors she ascribed to herself. She was convinced that her view of herself was his as well.

This encounter in the deli would not upset most people. In fact, most people would be delighted to run into an old acquaintance and chat for a few minutes. To Jane, however, this small incident became a crisis.

Because she has such a negative view of herself, she has difficulty believing others do not view her the same way.

The following is a list of potential triggering incidents for a self-esteem attack:

- Being reprimanded at work.

- Receiving a speeding ticket.

- Having someone not return our phone call.

- Saying something we regret saying.

- Perceiving that someone is staring at us.

- Performing any task inadequately.

- Thinking that we have made a crucial mistake.

- Being turned down for sex by our partner.

- Suspecting that we've done something strange or socially inappropriate.

- Experiencing any form of sarcasm or criticism directed at us.

- Feeling that someone has taken advantage of us.

- Thinking that someone is laughing at us.

- Sensing any form of rejection.

- Perceiving that we are being treated as insignificant or unimportant.

- Feeling unappreciated or disrespected.

- Perceiving that others discount our feelings.

- Feeling left out when others make plans and don't include us.

- Feeling that others don't listen to us.

Notice that in many of these potential triggering incidents merely "thinking," "sensing," or "perceiving" something to be happening can be enough to initiate the self-esteem attack.

Memory Loss

When the person with LSE is in the throes of a Self-Esteem Attack, his anxiety may be so great that he experiences periods of memory loss. He may be so upset that he does not hear what is being said to him and may have no memory afterwards of what he just said. He may not remember an entire conversation or incident at a later time. Usually, within a few minutes, the anxiety has subsided and he will be more calm and cognizant of what is happening around him, though he may never recall what occurred during those few seconds of extreme anxiety.

Example:

Jeremy attends a wedding where he is introduced to a woman he finds attractive and interesting. He decides he wants to ask her out but is afraid she will turn him down. After agonizing for several days, he finally musters the courage to call, telling himself that he can handle it if she declines. He has thought through exactly what he will say. When she answers, he says, "Hi, this is Jeremy, remember me? We met at the wedding Sunday." There is a long pause, after which she replies, "No, I don't remember you." Jeremy is stunned. She doesn't even remember him? He feels so foolish, so humiliated. "What can I do for you?" she asks. Jeremy is traumatized. He can't think of a thing to say. He can't even remember who he is talking to. He hears a voice talking to him but can't make sense of it. He hangs up the phone. Later when his anxiety sub-sides, he cannot remember what exactly either of them said or how the conversation ended. He feels embarrassed and berates himself for having made the call.

Example:

James is sitting in his first class of the new quarter; his instructor has just emphasized how important it is that every-one participate in the discussions, and she introduces a topic. As time passes, various students contribute their thoughts. James feels intense pressure to say something. He gets an idea and becomes absorbed in organizing his thoughts so that he can present it in an appropriate manner. Finally he raises his hand, is called on to speak, and makes his remark. Immediately he knows that something is wrong. Either he did not say what he intended to say or he has made some other terrible mistake because it has suddenly become very quiet and his classmates are staring at him. He feels devastated, wondering, but unable to remember exactly what he said.

James wants to run from the room but knows doing so will call even more attention to himself; he stays, and sits rigidly in his chair. He looks straight ahead or down at the table, never allowing his eyes to shift left or right, so as to avoid eye con-tact with anyone throughout the remainder of the class. Then he quickly slips out the door when class ends.

Because it is the beginning of a new quarter, James does not have any friends in the class. He feels there is no one he can talk to about the incident, so he never knows what he said—he has only his imagination to fill in the missing pieces.

These events are so painful and so truly terrifying that James and others with LSE are even more anxious and reluctant to participate the next time. Some may muster the courage to try again, especially if the stakes are high. Others will not have that courage; they may even take some drastic action: Jeremy may never again call a new acquaintance for a date, James may drop out of school. Anyone with LSE who has had such an experience may anguish over the incident for a long time; Jeremy will wonder what he said or did when he made his call, James will wonder what he really said and fear what others are thinking, finding the risk of asking someone too great.

James's fear arose from a situation that he perceived as negative, even terrifying: (1) speaking up and sharing opinions or ideas (2) with strangers (3) under circumstances where he was going to be evaluated (4) on an unfamiliar topic. This memory loss phenomenon is caused by extreme anxiety, which can be triggered by both positive and negative events.

Example:

Rick, who works for one of the largest computer companies in the nation, is named Worker-of-the-Year. While Rick is highly skilled at his work and consistently has innovative ideas, he is also quiet and self-effacing due to his LSE. Unable to personally recognize his worth to the company, this award comes as a complete shock. Equipped with a great sense of humor, he has gotten along well with his coworkers but generally has kept to himself and would never have anticipated receiving such an award.

At a scheduled company meeting, which included all employees and executives, the president, Ms Gregory, explained that she was there to announce the yearly award recipient, someone from the human resources department. The award winner would receive a plaque, a $5,000 bonus, and use of a new company car for one year.

She then began detailing the attributes of the person chosen. Everyone was excited, and the anticipation grew. When Ms. Gregory announced Rick's name, he froze in his seat, unable to believe that he had heard correctly—he actually went blank for a few seconds. When his head began to clear, he wondered why he could not remember whose name had been called.

Pandemonium had broken out in the room when Ms. Gregory announced Rick's name; those in attendance were on their feet cheering and clapping. It was then that he noticed everyone staring at him. As they started pushing him towards the front of the room, he realized he had not been dreaming after all. He was excited. He was overwhelmed. He was elated. He was also embarrassed to be the center of attention.

Ms. Gregory congratulated him, read the award, presented him with a set of car keys and a check, and told him there would be a reception following. She then asked Rick if she would like to say something.

Rick began talking. He evidently cracked several jokes that had his fellow workers laughing but Rick had no memory afterwards of what he had said. He didn't remember walking to the front of the room or even speaking; he only remembered their loud laughing and cheering. Afterwards, he felt frantic! Had he made a fool of himself? Had they all been laughing at him? What had he done?

At the reception, one after another of his colleagues came up to him, patted him on the back, and told him he had been great. As he began to calm down, he was, of course, pleased to receive the compliments and congratulations. He was also extremely relieved to realize that whatever he had said had evidently been acceptable, though he would always wonder exactly what it had been.

This type of incident leads to more self-doubt as individuals with LSE wonder and worry what else they might have said or what was said to them. They will never know unless they get feedback from someone who was present. Unfortunately, these distraught people are unlikely to solicit the information, since to do so would reveal their problem. Furthermore, if they did ask for feedback and were told they did fine, the person with LSE would probably not believe it.

The memory loss problem presents an enormous dilemma because the person is aware that others know what happened while he does not. Such incidents make those affected wonder about their sanity and make them doubly fearful of the next unexpected situation where they may suffer another bout of memory loss and have to deal with the consequences. Of course, these periods of memory loss do not mean a person is "crazy." What they do indicate, however, is the extent to which those with LSE experience anxiety, anxiety so severe that it produces this temporary amnesia.

Memory loss is a significant problem for those who suffer from LSE for the following reasons:

- The episode of memory loss is terrifying to experience, knowing we have no control over if or when it will occur.

- Our concerns about what happened during the period of memory loss will not be alleviated since we will never know for sure exactly what we did or said.

- Additional consequences may occur later as a result of not remembering the situation, i.e., others may make remarks about our behavior, others may ask questions about what we did or said, etc.

Partners of people with extremely low self-esteem become equally frustrated when they try to recap an argument or discussion and their partner says she has no recollection of it. Often the partner will not believe her and think she is trying to avoid discussing it or the partner may interpret this inability to recall "significant" conversations as a sign of disinterest in the relationship.

People with LSE may also "forget" specific happenings because they have "practiced" putting negative events out of their minds. Adults who grew up in very negative or traumatic environments may have used "forgetting" as a way of coping with continual emotional and/or physical abuse. Now that it has become a habit, they may "forget" any situation that is negative or just extremely stressful.

Whatever the cause, these experiences add to our devastation, humiliation, and despair when we are already battling LSE. Our anxiety and fear perpetuate a vicious emotional cycle that we are totally unable to monitor or control when our LSE is activated.

- *A note of comparison with those with healthy self-esteem:*

People with healthy self-esteem have not experienced bouts of debilitating emotions such as those described here as the result of self-esteem attacks. They, at times, get upset, angry, and sad, but these reactions are more moderate. They, too, experience situations that trigger reactions, but these situations are generally the result of negative dysfunctional behavior to which they are reacting appropriately. They are not triggered by seemingly normal everyday events. They do not experience periods of memory loss due to anxiety.

RECOVERY

Self-esteem attacks are the hallmark of low self-esteem. Everyone who suffers from LSE has them to some extent and every LSE sufferer, once aware of the pattern they take, can attest to the fact that their lives are in many ways controlled by these attacks. Self-esteem attacks can, however, be totally eliminated with commitment to a recovery program.

People with LSE can change the ways they respond to emotionally-packed, triggering events that culminate in a self-esteem attack though to do so takes time. Eventually, as they work through a program of recovery, they will find themselves thinking differently, as well as reacting less frequently and more moderately; they will also find that their emotional reactions don't last as long. When working on your self-esteem, mark your calendar each time you have a strong emotional reaction. Mark with a red pen if the reaction is extreme, orange if is moderate, blue if it is mild. Write in the length of time the reaction lasted. Occasionally look back at your calendar and note any changes in severity, frequency, or length of time it lasted. Awareness of our changing growth patterns provides encouragement and additional incentive to change.

Overcoming low slf-esteem and eliminating the ever debilitating self-esteem attacks are the goal of the Recovery Program Dr. Sorensen has developed. While not a quick fix, her program is effective for anyone who is highly motivated, persistent, and consistent in working the program. Dr. Sorensen conducts phone therapy with people around the globe.

THINGS TO DO

Exercise 1

It is important to recognize what triggers our emotional down-falls—the specific types of comments or events that "hook" us and cause a self-esteem attack. When we have distinguished what they are, we can begin to focus on the process by thinking, "Oh, there's one of those comments that usually upsets me" instead of just automatically reacting to it.

To identify your own triggers, try the following:

1. Think of the last time you experienced humiliation, devastation, or despair. Picture the incident. What were you doing? What was the occasion? Who was present? Where were you? How were you feeling before you became so distraught? What exactly happened? What did you do? Write all of this down.

2. Think back to other times when you have been upset. Visualize what was happening and what you were feeling. Try to determine what triggered your emotions. In the beginning, you may not be able to recognize your triggers until the incident has passed, and then only by looking back. In time you will be able to recognize the triggers when they come up.

3. In the future, each time you recognize that you are suffering from similar extreme emotions, try to identify what triggered them. Write this down and keep a record of the things that trigger you. Remember, awareness is the first step to developing new skills.

4. When you have identified a trigger, think through why it has become one for you. What does it mean to you? What does it say about you? Is it similar to situations from your childhood?

If so, what happened then? Write your answers in your note-book.

5. Look at your behaviors when you are triggered. What do you do? What do you say? (Note: Don't get down on yourself; that won't be helpful.) Write your answers in your notebook.

6. Continue to look for your triggers. Think of ways you could respond differently when triggered the next time. What could you say differently? What could you do differently? Write this down.

7. Visualize an interaction, substituting your new behaviors into the situation. Imagine yourself reacting differently than you have in the past. Picture yourself staying calm and composed. How does this feel? Write this down.

THINGS TO DO

Exercise 2

Your emotions are intense because of the degree of hurt you have experienced in the past. Even so, you can learn to control your reactions. Decide you are going to take control of your anxiety, so that when you feel it coming on, you can sidetrack it. This exercise is a step toward doing that.

1. When you feel that you are getting anxious, try saying calming statements to yourself. e.g., "It's going to be okay. Just stay calm. I'll be fine. I can do this."

2. Take several deep breaths. Try to relax into the chair where you are sitting or step outside and focus on breathing in the fresh air.

3. When you feel strong emotions surfacing, don't panic. Instead, tell yourself, "I can handle this. This will go away. I'm fine. I've gotten through this in the past."

4. If at all possible, avoid catastrophizing.

4

Ending the Self-Sabotage

JANE: procrastination

During the first two years that Jane worked for her present employer, she was required to make sales by phone. Although all salespeople struggle with the fear of rejection, Jane was immobilized by it. Still stinging from her divorce and her feelings of rejection, her confidence was at a low ebb. She dealt with her anxiety by avoiding and procrastinating on difficult tasks. She would drag herself to work and once there would busy herself with any mundane task she could find as she put off making the dreaded cold calls. Finally, with nothing left to distract her, she would force herself to the phone.

A self-defeating behavior is basically anything we say or do, or anything we fail to say or do, that is not in our own best interest or that defeats our own purpose. In this case, Jane avoids the job she has been hired to do, a practice that might ultimately prove self-defeating if it jeopardizes her reputation with the company. Like Jane, most individuals with low self-esteem both think and act in ways that are self-destructive and that sabotage their own goals.

Example:

> *Two of his coworkers invite Paris to go golfing with them on Saturday. Paris golfs weekly and would very much like to develop a friendship with each of them. However, he becomes anxious and worries that he may not be nearly as good as they are and may even make a fool of himself. He makes an excuse and doesn't go.*

Paris's refusal to go is a self-defeating behavior: he would like to become friends with his coworkers, but he surrenders to his fear and anxiety. When he decides to stay home, he is denying himself the opportunity to have what he wants. He defeats himself. Of course, Paris does not want to sabotage himself, nor is he even aware he is doing so. Rather, he is responding to the faulty video he has of his life and the irrational fears he has acquired as a result.

This video tells him that:

- He is probably not as good a golfer as his coworkers.

- He will probably make more bad shots than his coworkers.

- He will be embarrassed and feel he has made a fool of himself.

- Coworkers will notice his mistakes. They will remark or, at the very least, think negative thoughts about him and his abilities.

- They might pass these negative perceptions on to others.

- He will later be anxious when he sees them and other coworkers again.

- He will wonder each day which of his coworkers are talking about him and what they are saying.

As Paris considers these possibilities, which to him are *probabilities*, his anxiety and fear grow, eventually rendering him too frightened to accept the invitation.

That people act out in self-defeating ways and that they experience incredible pain are two crucial effects of low self-esteem. Both are present for Paris: he suffers from anxiety and is apprehensive, and as a result declines the invitation offered him. Paris might have had a different reaction if his coworkers had invited him to join them in a different activity. For example, if the invitation had been to go bowling and Paris perceives himself to be an outstanding bowler, he might have accepted. Another person with LSE might decline both invitations because she feels inadequate socially, while still others might accept both invitations out of fear of what the coworkers will think if they refuse. In this latter case, we may go, be miserable the entire time, but suffer through it because our reasoning tells us we have "no choice."

Here are some examples of ways we sabotage ourselves when we have low self-esteem:

- Lying, so no one will see our dysfunction.

- Calling in to work sick, when we aren't sick.

- Not applying for a job that we want.

- Not applying to college when we want to go.

- Procrastinating on anything that is very important to us.

- Remaining quiet when asked our opinion.

- Refusing to attend new events when we really desire to meet new people.

- Turning down an invitation when we really want to go.

- Isolating.

- Attacking another person in the middle of a self-esteem episode or attack.

- Not making our wants and needs known.

- Not sharing our true feelings.

- Not initiating with people we would like to spend time with.

- Not taking the risk to commit to a relationship.

- Not learning a new skill that we know we need.

These self-defeating behaviors are further complicated by their unpredictability. Each individual's video differs, so triggering events vary widely.

Let's look at another way Paris might have responded if the circumstances had been slightly altered and he had indeed participated.

Example:

Coworkers in Paris's office organize an office golf tournament. The plan is for everyone to play, with a dinner afterwards. Paris, who in fact plays golf most weekends with his brother, feels inadequate socially, especially in groups. He feels, however, that he must participate or his coworkers will ridicule him, though they have never done so before.

The day of the tournament Paris is filled with anxiety. He has not slept well because of worrying that he will perform badly and embarrass himself. Since he is anxious, he does indeed play far below his normal game. He feels humiliated; he imagines that others are laughing at him. Several others are playing more poorly than Paris, but he doesn't notice. He wishes the day were over, and he descends into a depression as it goes on. He becomes quiet and lethargic. Seeing that he is discouraged, his coworkers try to joke with him and encourage him, but Paris only feels more dejected, realizing that they have seen his reaction.

At the dinner, Paris eats very little. He tries to make small talk, but inside he is devastated and finds it difficult to focus on the conversation. As dessert is served, Paris feigns illness and leaves. Throughout the weekend, he berates himself and continues to dwell on the day of golf. He is still deeply depressed on Monday and calls in to work saying he has the flu—though he feels certain that no one believes him.

When he returns to work on Tuesday, he dreads facing everyone and has difficulty making eye contact. He knows he is acting strangely and imagines that everyone is thinking he is weird but is unable to control his emotions or behave differently.

As in Paris's case, some people do not benefit from advice to "just do it; you'll feel better if you do." Self-criticism and reactions to imagined criticism from others can undermine the benefits of participation. No matter how he responds, Paris distorts the situation in his mind, creating anxiety that serves as a prelude to self-defeating behaviors.

Paris is caught in the vicious cycle of LSE. Having repeatedly experienced anxiety, embarrassment, and humiliation that accompany self-esteem attacks, he apprehensively anticipates the next event that will trigger these feelings. When any new incident arises, he is programmed to accept it as another opportunity to fail. His subsequent actions are guided by his need to avoid fear and pain, motives that do not produce rewarding results. In taking defensive action, Paris again feels defeated. He lives in dread of the next situation he must face. Each new situation becomes part of a self-perpetuating cycle.

Days later, when Paris is feeling better, he may be able to see how irrational he was. He may recognize that he magnified the situation, reacting out of proportion to the incident. This awareness, however, may provoke yet another cycle of depression if he berates himself for his overreaction, telling himself he "should" have been able to handle the situation "better." Then again, there may be days, weeks, or months when Paris responds in a more healthy fashion, if he is feeling less vulnerable. He may be less anxious, at ease with others, able to laugh at himself, feeling less threatened. He may be busily and successfully occupied with the normal demands of daily living, temporarily free from inner conflict, until the next event triggers his self-doubts. In other words, people with LSE are not always hypersensitive or fearful; they frequently have periods when they are not so threatened, especially if they have experienced recent successes and feel approval from those around them.

- *A note of comparison with those with healthy self-esteem:*

People with healthy self-esteem do not perform self-defeating behaviors on a regular basis, as do those with LSE. Instead, they generally do the things they want to, strive toward their goals, and do not constantly agonize over their decisions. They readily enjoy new experiences and accept invitations without fear. The exception to this rule: introverts with healthy self-esteem do not prefer to participate in large groups whether or not they know the people involved and may turn down invitations to large group activities when they feel they can do so without repercussions.

Let's revisit Jane and look at how her low self-esteem and subsequent self-defeating behaviors affected her relationship with John, her ex-husband. These behaviors influence any relationship when one of the partners suffers from feelings of inadequacy.

JANE: relying on John

Jane has, of course, suffered from LSE all her life—for it is a problem that begins in childhood. Prior to meeting and marrying John, however, her low self-esteem was latent; she had not suffered a self-esteem attack for some time. She had surrounded herself with positive people, was succeeding in school, and was doing well at her job; she was also spending less time with her critical family. The one exception to feeling content was that she remained single and felt alone.

Family and friends continually asked her if she was dating or "had someone special" in her life. She felt pressure from these questions. Wanting to be coupled, Jane began engaging in what would later become a pattern of self-defeating behaviors. She felt she "needed" to be in a relationship—that finding someone who loved her would make her whole.

When she met John, Jane saw him as a good "catch" in every way. She was attracted to him and soon realized that the attraction was mutual. When she was with him, she felt less needy. She told herself that if such a powerful, attractive, intelligent, and ambitious man wanted her, she must be important and attractive too. By attaching herself to him, she felt better about herself.

Feeling truly desirable for the first time in her life, Jane willingly began changing, attempting to mold herself into the woman she thought John wanted. She changed her style of dress and altered her schedule. She gave up activities, friends, and interests seemingly unaware that doing so was not in her best interest. She became obsessed with pleasing John—no sacrifice

was too great. In trying to capture his devotion, Jane was los-
ing herself; she no longer thought about what she wanted but
instead conformed to his opinions and wishes.

When they married, Jane quit her job, giving up her only
remaining contact with the outside world. She continued to put
all of her energy into meeting John's needs while denying her
own. Relying solely on John to provide meaning for her life,
Jane became even more needy. However, John, who had been
demanding and domineering, no longer liked the new person he
had sculpted; he felt smothered by Jane's neediness and reacted
by distancing from her. As he backed away, Jane moved
towards him, becoming more possessive. She began to feel des-
perate. She continued pursuing him, he continued retreating;
finally the relationship deteriorated completely.

Like all of us, Jane needs affirmation and companionship. She
needs to feel understood, to feel she has worth, to feel loved and
lovable. During college, she had built solid friendships that provided many of these needs; a nagging question remained, however,
as to whether someone would ever want her as a life partner. This
longing to be loved and to believe herself lovable made Jane vulnerable; as a "needy" person, she was ripe for the picking. When
John came along, his many truly positive qualities made him
look like a knight in shining armor; finally, Jane had the opportunity for fulfillment through John.

Lacking confidence in herself and with limited experience in
intimate relationships, Jane followed John's lead. When he
assertively stated his wants and needs, she was there ready to
accommodate him. When he gave advice, she followed it explicit-
ly. When he stated his opinions, she deferred. Jane believed John
was superior to her—more capable than she was at deciding what
was best for her; she subsequently relinquished her own power,
allocating responsibility for her happiness to John. She felt in need
of someone to love her, someone to be focused on her, building
her up emotionally, and convincing her she had worth. She

appointed John as the "supplier" of her needs. The more she relied on him to direct her through life, the more dependent she became on him. The more she abdicated her personal power, the more needy she became, with little or no self-confidence remaining.

Rigidity

Some people cope with their self-esteem issues by becoming overly rigid. Motivated by fear and past hurtful experiences, these people close themselves off from new experiences and opportunities to develop new skills, another form of self-sabotage. Without realizing they are doing so, they grasp one idea or way to do things and then close themselves off from any additional input that might actually improve their performance or enhance their perspective. For example, a man is now working in his father's company and suggests to his father several changes that he feels will modernize their business. His father feels criticized, becomes rigid and defensive, and tells his son that the way he has run the company has been effective so far and he sees no need to change things now.

These inflexible people operate as though to accept new insight would be to admit failure in "not knowing" in the first place; they seem to see anyone who challenges their position, as questioning their self-worth or competence. These people tend to resist focusing on self-improvement; they are not open to suggestions or constructive criticism, rarely take classes or read to gain new insights. They are in a sense immovable objects.

People with this degree of rigidity tend to be opinionated, frequently advocating beliefs and behaviors that are outmoded or clearly inaccurate and nonproductive. They generally defer to those they see as authorities, placing more confidence even in total strangers than they do in themselves, allowing their lives to be directed by someone just because of his or her position of importance. At the same time they reject suggestions from those close to them, interpreting this input as some type of threat.

Gravitating to others who are equally rigid, these people are vulnerable to recruitment by cults and religions that encourage obedience and unquestioning belief in dogmas. Such authoritarian groups provide security in concrete, specific, and unchanging "rules" or "truth" around which insecure people can mold their lives. They feel safe in groups that teach that there is a right and wrong way to do everything, providing fixed beliefs and standards that the person with LSE can cling to. Discouraging people from thinking for themselves, these organizations clone their followers, dictating what they should do arid say, who they should associate with, and even how they should look and dress, thus providing a predictable and static blueprint for the insecure person to live by.

Rigidity, while common place for those with LSE, is another form of self-defeating behavior because it interferes with cognitive and emotional growth, encourages us to be closed to new ideas and perspectives, distances us from intimate relationships, and deprives us of our individuality. This limited form of thinking can stifle careers and create obstinate and uninteresting people whom others desire to avoid because they are so closed. Instead of being open to new experiences, eager to face new challenges, desirous of self-improvement, and interested in diverse and fresh ways of thinking, these rigid people remain stagnant, continually focused on the same issues throughout their lives, never moving forward.

Many with low self-esteem cling to childhood information and traditions, unwilling to accept a changing world. Fearful of change and self-focused, they think "it has always been done this way, and that means it is the only right way." Change would disrupt their ability to categorize everything, to stereotype others and their behaviors, and this thinking ultimately leads to an "Us" and "Them" mentality of believing that resisting change is what's best for them and therefore what's best for others. It's basically the belief that I and the people who think like me know what's right and best for everyone else. Because of their rigidity, the thinking of the LSE sufferer may go in this direction: "Because I've always believed something to be right, it can't possibly be just one of many feasible choices. If it's right for me, it's what's right for everyone." In other words, in their desperate need to be right and to feel secure, they seem locked into believing that they know best how others should think and live. Many even take the position of believing that those who think and do things differently are wrong, bad, or even potentially dangerous to society and to their lives. They would prefer to have behavior dictated by laws or by a society that agrees with them. They fully fail to recognize that progress is generally only achieved because of new ideas, new ways of thinking, fresh opinions. So, the feeling is "If I even consider that others could have a different but acceptable opinion or lifestyle, it means I won't know what's right or wrong. Others might choose to live differently than I do. I would have to accept them and their ideas. I wouldn't be able to control them. I feel better when we keep everything simple, with rules about what's right and wrong, good and bad, so that I know what to do and so that we keep others in line."

To these extremely insecure people, allowing too many choices means they wouldn't have "the" answer: because there is no one right answer. They wouldn't be able to impose their view on others or to control the behavior of others. This is most disconcerting to the person who feels a need to have an environment that remains predictable, that he understands, and that he agrees with. Thus, suggesting that most of life is individual choice is threatening. It means allowing others to be themselves and that means tolerance and options. To the LSE sufferer, options are confusing. Which one is the best one? What should I tolerate? What should I criticize? What should I accept? Allowing for differences in the behavior and traditions of others means letting go of this rigid thinking. Instead, those with low self-esteem often remain intolerant and rigid, judging others and becoming undesirable companions to those who accept change, who relish options, who value individual freedom, and who believe that most of life should be personal choice.

Example:

Marvin and Kyle have been married for three years. Both have budding careers in the sporting goods industry and both are active athletically, one of the main things they have in common. Kyle has many friends while Marvin is less socially skilled and suffers from low self-esteem. Over the past two months, Kyle has expressed an interest in and then began attending Buddhist meditation sessions with two women she recently befriended at work. Marvin is bothered by this. He was raised Catholic and he thinks that this is not something Kyle should be doing. At first he remains quiet, thinking that she probably won't keep it up. Instead, he sees her becoming more and more interested and tells her that he disapproves and doesn't want her to continue. Kyle becomes angry and accuses Marvin of trying to control who she is rather than respecting her right to make her own decisions. She suggests that he seems satisfied with the repetition in his life but that she is excited about new opportunities to learn new things and have new experiences. She tells him that she would have preferred if he had asked her what it meant to her and what she was getting out of it rather than making a judgment and then thinking that he has the right to dictate what she can do. She also thinks he is only objecting because he doesn't understand what she is doing and is unwilling to do or consider anything different from what his parents taught him. Marvin is taken aback. He has never considered himself to be closed to new opportunities but rather a person who knows right from wrong.

Kyle and Marvin have very different perspectives. Marvin is frightened by seeing Kyle become involved in something that he doesn't understand. Rather than try to discuss it with her so as to gain some insight into what she is doing and why, he makes a judgment based on old messages that tell him things that are different or unusual must be wrong. He doesn't respect Kyle's ability to make good choices for herself and tries to force her to quit something just because he is unfamiliar with it and therefore suspicious of it. This is a typical reaction from a person with low self-esteem who is fearful of the unknown and the unpredictable, and anything that isn't in his personal rulebook. Marvin's confrontation is also an attempt to keep Kyle from getting involved in things that he doesn't know about, that would make him uncomfortable, or that would leave him feeling left out. He maintains his sense of security within himself and within the relationship by maintaining a lifestyle that is predictable and constant, and he expects Kyle to do the same.

Example:

Selma shares with her husband, Tim, that she had lunch today with Hank, who works at the Animal Shelter, where she has started to do volunteer work. She has mentioned Hank before, sharing how good he is with animals and how nice he has been to her. Tim is not pleased and shows it. When Selma asks what is wrong, Tim lets her know that he doesn't approve of her having lunch with a person who she knows is gay. Selma just stares at him for a few seconds. "Are you kidding me?" she asks. "You don't want me to have lunch with Hank because he's gay?" She can't believe what she just heard. "He's been the nicest to me since I began volunteering there. He's interesting, he's fun, and so what if he's gay? I'd think you'd be relieved? You're so jealous and he certainly won't be hitting on me. I thought you told me you weren't prejudiced like your father."

Selma and Tim continued to argue about Hank and about Selma being friends with him. Selma was shocked to find out that Tim was prejudiced about how another person lived his life and that Tim thought he had the right to tell her that she should feel similarly. Tim is insecure and has often been jealous and critical of her friends and activities. She told Tim that she

would choose her own friends and that she was disappointed
that he would be so judgmental about something that had no
affect on him personally and certainly no affect on their own
relationship.

This is but another example of how people who feel insecure and who have rigid beliefs are intolerant of the beliefs of others as though others' differing perspectives somehow impose on their own lives. They prefer to see life as having rules, standards, and beliefs that everyone must adhere to, thus reducing their responsibility to decide what is right for themselves and them alone. They fear making the wrong choices and so want choices to be legislated so that they are safe. They fear those who choose differently. Tim has rigid beliefs that he obtained in childhood about what is acceptable and what is not. Consequently, not only does he have opinions of what is right for him, but he feels equally adamant that others should believe similarly. He doesn't like it when his wife not only has a very different view but is unhappy with what she labels as prejudice and intolerance. He thinks that his family and friends will think less of him when they learn that his wife has a gay friend. He hopes they will never find out. He is bothered by what he sees as an increasingly independent and bothersome streak in Selma that he labels as getting on the "wrong path." He feels nervous and agitated. He needs the support of Selma to feel secure about who he is and what he believes.

Sadly, those with LSE who become so rigid cheat themselves of the pleasures, and happiness of life. They do not allow themselves to see life from all perspectives; they do not engage in aspects of life beyond their own small community circle. They are frequently uninterested, uninformed, and uninvolved in social issues beyond those that impact them directly, once again limiting their contact and their opportunity to view other perspectives of their world.

Getting Needs Met Through Others

The drive to get their needs met by others is typical of people with low self-esteem because they have not developed the inner resources to nurture themselves, nor are they creative in getting their needs met by themselves. They do not respect or love themselves sufficiently. Without self-love, those with LSE do not believe in their ability to get their wants and needs met from within; instead, they try to find happiness by attaching themselves to someone they love and admire. Placing their future in the hands of someone else, submitting and deferring, they surrender the right and opportunity to choose for themselves and to chart their own path in life.

When Jane attached herself to John, she had certain expectations of him. She assumed he had her best interests at heart, and she put him "in charge" of her life, relinquishing her right to make her own choices. This hierarchy of John dominating and Jane submitting expanded to their entire relationship. John, too, was needy and took the dominating route—telling Jane what to do, demanding that his needs get met. Later when Jane expected him to reciprocate by meeting her needs, he did not respond; he continued to focus on himself.

When suffering with LSE, we may even inaccurately believe that someone else can meet all of our needs. Since we believe our partner "knows" the things we do not, we assume our relationship with this exceptional person should sustain us. We think we do not need other friends or activities in our life. We adore, maybe even idolize, this person: he or she is all we need.

Submitting to the wishes of someone else frees us from the responsibility and the possibility of making a mistake, which others might see. By placing our trust in someone we respect and admire, we do not have to deal with the constant fear and anxiety that accompanies decision-making for the LSE sufferer. Thus, the process of attaching ourselves to another person makes us feel "safe"; we can't make the wrong decision if we aren't making any decisions at all.

Jane did what John asked of her and expected him to reciprocate. When he did not adhere to the same rules he had set for her, she demanded his time and companionship, she demanded understanding, and she demanded affirmation. These demands, of course, produced the opposite result; the disciple does not make demands of the master. John, who once seized the opportunity to be Jane's guardian, critic, and advisor, felt no indebtedness to Jane; he was completely unaware of the connection between the demands he had placed on her and her present emotional state. The roles had been agreed upon; John had no compunction about the arrangement and he had no need to change.

Jane believed John should reciprocate all that she gave because she had convinced herself that she did these things "for John," when in truth, Jane did the things she did "to get" attention, affirmation, affection—to get her needs met. These are the actions of a needy person.

Behaviors we use that demonstrate our neediness include:

- Being preoccupied with a person from the time we meet. Continuing to be preoccupied, seeing ourselves only as an extension of this person.

- Being shocked that an attractive, intelligent person would find us worthy of his or her attention.

- Giving up our friends, our interests, our goals to spend time with another person.

- Staying home so we won't miss a call from a new acquaintance instead of leading an active life of our own.

- Doing things for another person that aren't asked for or expected in order to get that person to like us.

- Consistently deferring to the wishes of others, placing more importance on meeting their needs than our own.

- Taking on the ideas and beliefs of others without first considering their merit.

Neediness is not very attractive. In fact, the attempts of a needy person to get his needs met, in the way Jane did with John, usually produce the opposite result. The partner may feel revolted or manipulated; he may also feel responsible for the needy person in ways he does not want to. In time, Jane's behavior made John feel angry and smothered; in time, it eroded their already dysfunctional marriage.

Because of the emptiness they feel within themselves, needy people also have difficulty being alone. When alone, they feel they are communing with someone who is inadequate and unimportant, so time spent by themselves only magnifies their neediness. Consequently, they feel desperate to be in a relationship—any relationship—and will settle for much less than is healthy for them. Of course, these people do not recognize the fact that when they do not value themselves, others won't value them either.

In their frantic search to find someone who will supply their ongoing needs, people with LSE often go through a rapid succession of partners, desperately wanting to feel loved. They frequently become addicted to the "beginnings" of relationships when couples are most affectionate, exclusive, and demonstrative towards one another. In that early stage of a relationship, they experience wonderful feelings of love and acceptance and are convinced that finally they have found the right person—the person who will bridge the gap to fulfillment. Having made a hasty commitment to this new acquaintance, however, they soon experience unhappiness once again as infatuation wears off and they see this individual in a truer light.

The process is similar to focusing with a zoom lens and later switching to a wide angle lens. At first, the needy person sees this new friend as her lifeline. Since the two happy people spend all of their time together, focus only on each other, and ignore other demands in their lives, this relationship seems the answer to her prayers. The two have fun, talk incessantly, and explore together, cut off from the world. This infatuation period, while normal in the beginning of a relationship, is not representative of real life and cannot continue indefinitely. As the couple gradually returns their attention to other obligations, family, interests, and friends, the broader picture comes into view. This is the point of disillusionment for the person with low self-esteem, when she sees that her new partner is not available or willing to constantly respond to her abundant needs. She then repeats the same interactions that ruined the last full-time relationship, with little or no insight as to how she herself destroys the very things she wants. Instead, this person with LSE expresses disappointment in her new companion, blaming him for changing. She does not recognize that she has sabotaged yet another relationship; instead, she views this new partner as purposefully withholding what she needs. In her self-focused neediness, she does not realize that she is simply asking too much.

Her internal video is inaccurate; due to distorted, subjective thinking, the person with LSE views life and the behaviors of others from a skewed perspective. Others are to blame for his unhappiness. This person may not take time to grieve the end of one relationship before his desperation leads him to search for another, convinced that only a relationship can fill the void he feels inside—and so the cycle continues.

Some who experience this neediness don't have the courage or self-confidence to engage in dating relationships at all. They may not even know how to develop friendships. They have often experienced rejection in the past, and lacking insight into the possible causes, they are too fearful to approach potential companions or initiate positive interaction. Still others will remain in abusive relationships, too fearful of being alone to leave; too doubtful of their ability to take care of themselves to venture out on their own.

• *A note of comparison with those with healthy self-esteem:*

People with healthy self-esteem do not rely on others to get their needs met but attempt to be self-sufficient by finding a variety of means to fulfill their needs. They try to maintain support systems that include people with whom they can confide, people who share similar interests, and people with similar values. They know that no one person can meet their needs and they do not have that expectation.

Intolerance is not compatible with healthy self-esteem and so those who feel secure in themselves are less likely to be rigid in their acceptance of others, realizing that as long as the choices and individual differences of others do not affect them negatively, everyone has a right to decide for themselves who they are and what they believe. They are secure in the life choices that they have made consciously and with considerable thought.

Also, those with healthy self-esteem do not want to defer their choices and decisions to others but value the freedom and accompanying responsibility that enables them to be in charge of their own lives.

Two Extremes: Noisy Reactors and Quiet Reactors

When anxious, frightened, or attacked, people respond with a variety of defensive styles. People with low self-esteem may react like injured animals, by hiding and trying to be invisible; these are the Quiet Reactors. Others try to gain respect and approval by showing others they have intellect, opinions, skills; often these people do so in the more boisterous fashion of Noisy Reactors. Both can be extreme, as illustrated below.

Figure 2: Two Extremes: Noisy and Quiet Reactors

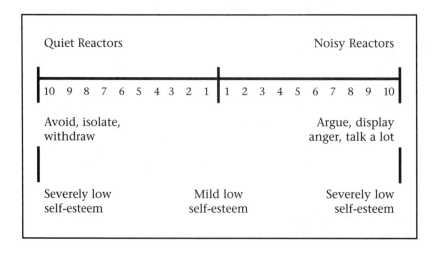

Noisy Reactors

Those who become noisy when anxious often talk too fast, too loud, too forcefully, or merely laugh a lot. They are nervous and feel a need to participate even though they may not have much to say, even when they aren't informed on the subject. In their noisy fashion, they talk too much and may even monopolize the conversation, eager to talk about themselves, or at least get attention.

All people want recognition and acceptance; those with LSE especially need to feel they "fit in." However, coming from dysfunctional backgrounds, they may have received little or poor training in social skills and may not know how to appropriately assert themselves. In their extreme insecurity and their desire to get attention, they may inappropriately blurt out their opinions too strongly or at an inopportune moment. They may plunge into the middle of a conversation before getting a total grasp of the situation or the direction of the interaction, unknowingly eliciting negative reactions. So focused on participating and getting attention, they may also interrupt others or talk over them. They have a need to be the center of attention and in their exuberance make very poor listeners; they later are hurt when people don't seek out their company. These Noisy Reactors are often seen as insensitive, obnoxious, and rude.

Unlike Quiet Reactors, who try not to be noticed, Noisy Reactors may express themselves or attempt to get attention in nonverbal ways, such as dressing in unconventional, gaudy, or flamboyant clothes. Like so many of the actions of those with LSE, this usually does not garner positive results, especially among adults. When their attempts to get noticed bring negative responses, Noisy Reactors become angry—and react in their noisy fashion. They set up a situation that will most likely attract disapproval and then feel rejected when that disapproval comes—another form of self-defeating behavior.

Some Noisy Reactors also express their noisy quality by being argumentative, disagreeable, even attacking. They can be verbally aggressive, confrontational and demanding, creating interminable fights. They may yell and throw tantrums. Frequently feeling slighted by others, especially when they are not getting attention, they nag, complain constantly, and punish their partners. Basically, Noisy Reactors are those who, when wounded, shoot from the hip, convinced their perceptions are accurate.

Noisy Reactors frequently have stormy, often chaotic relationships unless their partners are very passive and submissive. For a time, these partners may put tremendous energy into pleasing and placating their noisy reactor, while setting aside their own needs; not knowing what else to do, they actually reward and encourage this inappropriate behavior. Other partners get drawn into arguments by the Noisy Reactor, arguments that can erode the relationship.

Example:

> *Terry and Jo have been married two years. Jo is insecure in the relationship; questioning Terry's commitment to her, she suspiciously watches for inconsistencies in his behavior or contradictions to his promises. She sees each action or word from him as an indication of how he feels about her. When he is too tired to make love, she interprets this as his losing interest in her; when he is grouchy, she thinks he is unhappy with her.*
>
> *Terry is an accountant and works long days near tax time. Jo is a golf pro at a local course; her slowest times at work are in the winter, when Terry is beginning his busy season. On a day in February, Terry comes home late from work for the second day in a row. As soon as he enters, Jo snaps at him, "So, what have you been up to tonight? Don't you like spending the evenings with me anymore?" Terry stares at her and says, "I told you this morning I would probably be late. You know my*

work is picking up—it's that time of the year, remember?"
Ignoring his explanation, Jo snaps again, "Right. So, where did
you eat dinner and who did you go with?" Terry angrily replies,
"For your information, I haven't had dinner. In fact, I worked
through the dinner hour thinking maybe we'd go get a pizza,
but forget that. I'll just make myself a sandwich."

Realizing Terry's intense anger, Jo begins to panic. What is
he thinking? Is he fed up with her? Doesn't she have the right
to ask where he had been? "I think pizza's a good idea," Jo
says, but Terry just shakes his head. "What's the matter? Why
can't we go get a pizza?" Jo asks. "I'm out of the mood now,"
Terry says and walks out of the room.

Jo feels abandoned. The rest of the evening she is despondent.
What did she do that was so terrible? Why is he so unreasonable?
After all, she has a right to be angry. He didn't even empty the
dishwasher this morning, which he had promised he would do. In
fact, there are a lot of other things he doesn't follow through on.
What does this all mean? She doesn't know whether to confront
him about these things or whether she should just be quiet since
he is so angry.

Jo builds up anger when she sees that Terry doesn't always do
things on her time schedule, like emptying the dishwasher. As her
anger grows, she becomes irrational and suspicious, imagining
other transgressions, interpreting them to mean he doesn't care
about her. She feels justified in her reaction and confronts Terry,
who is oblivious to any problem. Repeatedly experiencing Jo's distrust, Terry becomes disgusted with her. When he responds with
anger rather than remorse, Jo becomes anxious, questioning both
his actions and her own. She is unable to digest his explanation and
disregards it, totally focused on her own seemingly justified doubts.
Nothing gets resolved, and both are left feeling disillusioned.

In therapy, those with LSE are often obsessed with finding
answers for the behavior of their partners. They repeatedly ask the
therapist, "Why is he doing this? What do you think it means when

he/she...?" Any answer they get that does not match their preconceived conclusions is discounted. They block out all information except that which confirms their suspicions. When the partner has distanced herself, they become obsessed with how to get the partner's attention back, though they continue to harbor feelings of betrayal. They are unable to see what actually caused the problem in the first place—their own low self-esteem.

In extreme cases, some Noisy Reactors turn their anger and aggression on themselves. These actions can take the form of physical abuse of their bodies or destruction of their own property. They may also engage in other forms of irresponsible and self-defeating behavior; they may abruptly quit a job or spend money allocated for bills—all in an attempt to find immediate relief or pleasure that will override their pain.

Over time, Noisy Reactors may experience many altercations with others, especially with those in positions of authority. Even when genuinely attempting to be assertive, Noisy Reactors can be aggressive and may be viewed by others as contentious, contrary, short-tempered, and difficult to get along with. Others who are not as aggressive may be perceived as overbearing and selfish. All of this noisy behavior is really a well disguised cry for help, for approval and acceptance. Unfortunately, it is not easily recognized as such.

Although a response is aggressive, it can actually result from passive behavior on the part of the person with low self-esteem. If this person has been hurt but does not feel able to confront the perpetrator of the perceived offense, she will store up this hurt until, like a volcano erupting, it all comes pouring out—usually as a response to a far less significant offense.

Example:

> *Marcy and Joan have agreed to have lunch together once a week, choosing a new restaurant each time. Because they come from opposite directions in the city, they drive separately and meet at the chosen location. Marcy is very conscious of time and is always prompt for these luncheon dates. Joan is usually late, her tardiness sometimes extending to a half hour. Marcy is irritated by Joan's lateness and sees it as a sign of disrespect; she is, however, afraid to share her feelings with Joan. When Joan arrives, she does not apologize for being late but acts as if there is no problem, angering Marcy all the more.*
>
> *For seven weeks Marcy's hostility toward Joan has grown until when once again, Joan enters the restaurant 10 minutes late, Marcy rises and shouts, "Well, you finally made it. I'm leaving. I'm tired of waiting on you every week. You are the most inconsiderate person I've ever met."*
>
> *Joan is taken aback. She looks at her watch and says, "I'm only ten minutes late. Why are you reacting like this? What's wrong with you?" Marcy, near tears, shakes her head and rushes out of the restaurant, angry and humiliated.*

Marcy's response is not the behavior of an aggressive person; instead, her actions are those of a passive person who has held in her anger rather than express it immediately. Had she confronted Joan the first time, her reaction would not have been so explosive. She could have calmly shared her feelings about not wanting to spend time waiting. By being passive, however, and holding in her feelings until her emotions are out of control, she is reacting to eight weeks of increasing anger, as she moves from a simmering anger at Joan to a seething rage.

As in this example, when the passive person finally erupts, her behavior is out of proportion to the present infraction, for indeed the venom that pours forth is a reaction to the entire period of neglect. Marcy's outburst and behavior receive negative attention from both Joan and others in the eatery while Joan innocently looks on, totally perplexed. In addition, Marcy's actions enable Joan to focus on the inappropriateness of Marcy's behavior rather than deal with the real issue of her persistent tardiness. Joan may later apologize to Marcy but, in the process, may suggest that Marcy really should have told her sooner how she felt. This once again throws the responsibility back on Marcy, who will be even more reluctant to confront someone in the future. (This sort of passive behavior as well as aggressive, assertive, and passive-aggressive behavior is explored in detail in Chapter 9.)

Passivity

Passivity produces Noisy Reactors in yet another way. Sometimes people like Marcy do not confront the Joans in their life; instead, they go home fully enraged and attack the first person there who crosses their path. This happens if Joan is in a position of authority, for instance, Marcy's supervisor; confronting Joan then might result in dire consequences. In a case where confronting the offending person could have serious repercussions, a person with LSE may hold in the anger and direct it at an unsuspecting—and undeserving—family member because reprisal is less likely. (If exploding towards a family member is not an option, this outburst may occur in the presence of a trusted friend or coworker.) Thus, many Noisy Reactors endure rage until it builds to the point where they explode, directing their anger at someone totally innocent. Learning to be assertive can correct this problem (see Chapter 9).

Determining the source of the anger that a person with LSE displays can be difficult. He may carry around a lingering rage from repeated abuse as a child, when he was powerless to change his circumstances. Now when someone treats him in a way that resembles the past mistreatment, he explodes without warning, completely taking the other person by surprise. These unresolved and lingering memories become the triggers or activating events in our lives, the buttons that—when pushed—send us into unpredictable emotional backlashes.

The unsuspecting person on the receiving end of one of these verbal barrages finds the outburst confusing, to say the least. Believing these attacks represent the true feelings and thoughts of her friend or loved one, she takes very personally (personalizes) the things being said about her and to her. Once she has personalized the outburst, she is also "hooked" (drawn into) the episode, entering the fray in an attempt to defend herself and clarify the situation. She may respond angrily and with criticism, ridiculing her attacker. While understandable, this response only serves to exacerbate the situation, upsetting the person with LSE even more. These altercations can then easily deteriorate into chaos, leaving both people alienated and questioning the relationship.

When bombarded by a person with low self-esteem, others will simply express disgust and threaten to leave. This sets the Noisy Reactor into a panic as she responds to feelings of abandonment. And so the situation continues to snowball, becoming increasingly chaotic.

What the person with LSE really needs in these moments of doubt is reassurance that she is loved. She is really asking the question, "Do you care about me? Am I important to you? If so, why are you treating me this way?" If the partner can remain "unhooked" and reassure the Noisy Reactor that she is loved, if the partner can explain that the inconsistency was an oversight or mistake, not an intentional slight, and just apologize, the problem will dissipate quickly. The person with LSE will almost instantly calm down and will likely be remorseful about her outburst. Without this reassurance, however, she will most probably continue to be suspicious of her partner's true intentions.

Quiet Reactors

Quiet Reactors respond differently, shutting down emotionally. They withdraw, isolate, or just remain silent so they do not say or do anything to draw attention in a way that would ultimately embarrass them. Deep inside they want to participate and share in the experience as they see others doing, for they feel out of place all the while they are looking on. Their anxiety can become so great that they feel tongue-tied; when asked a direct question, they may stammer or say they don't know, even when they think they do, because the fear of being wrong is so great. If they do perchance respond and do so appropriately, they will still be uncertain if they have performed adequately. They become even more quiet as they try to discern the reaction of others, possibly wondering for hours or days if what they said was okay.

Because Quiet Reactors feel inadequate, they may have actually practiced being invisible, staying in the background, and deferring to others: they are unaware of this acquired pattern of behavior and how it negatively affects their lives. They do not understand that it is largely through communication with others, through sharing and receiving, that we gain new information and ways of looking at things that help us to learn and ultimately to have the insight to know who we are and who we want to be. Those who close themselves off from others deprive themselves of the experience of relating and the tools that come with it over time. Also, it is through interaction with others that we reveal enough about ourselves to new acquaintances that they see our character and the attributes that spark interest. Those with LSE, however, are too fearful to let others see who they are; they are unsure of what they think and feel, and they are afraid that they might say the wrong thing or reveal their lack of knowledge. They also shy away from any conversation that involves controversy, fearing disapproval or reprisal. As they hide from others in this way, they do become invisible—people who are present but not heard; people who are lonely but who don't know how to relate; people who feel others don't respect them; people who feel insignificant—-and while attempting to play it safe, only hurt themselves. Out of self-protection, they do not reveal enough about themselves to new acquaintances to demonstrate their good traits or spark interest. They have practiced being invisible for so long they are unsure of who they really are.

So attuned are they to wanting to be like everyone else in the ways considered essential that Quiet Reactors with LSE do not allow themselves to recognize or claim their original thoughts, utilize their creativity, or develop their ideas. They are also unable to trust their perceptions or beliefs. They consciously attempt to be noncontroversial in speech; thus, they are less likely to be criticized. They make every effort to dress conservatively and in neutral colors; thus, they are less likely to be noticed. They diligently, rigidly, and specifically follow the rules; thus, they are less likely to be caught in some offense. All of this is an attempt to be invisible: If no one notices them, they can't be viewed as unusual or strange. They learn to meld into the crowd.

Example:

Breta, a lonely young single woman, decides to attend a community single's function she has heard about: a speaker with reception to follow. Anxiously, she gets ready and drives to the event, but when she arrives, she is too fearful to enter. Breta sits in her car for a while and then returns home. Once there, she chastises herself for being such a "wimp" and decides to go back. In the parking lot where the meeting is to take place, her confidence again wavers. She sits in her car for another five minutes, finally getting out and entering the building. By now she is late; the meeting has begun. She enters the room noticing that some eyes are diverted from the speaker toward her. She is embarrassed for arriving late and slinks into the back row, sitting away from everyone else in attendance. When the speaker finishes, some people gravitate to the front of the room

*while others amble toward the refreshments. Not spotting any-
one she knows, Breta stands on the fringes of the activity, avoiding eye contact; she feels too awkward and self-conscious to
approach anyone. As soon as she gets the courage to move,
Breta heads for the door and runs to her car. There she bursts
into tears and vows she will never do anything like this again.
She feels humiliated and devastated and even more alone. She
is unaware that her self-defeating behaviors have contributed to
her unsuccessful attempts to fit in and meet people.*

Quiet Reactors try to be in places where they will not be
noticed, making it a practice to sit to the side or back in meetings
or group functions, always staying on the periphery of the action.
They avoid making eye contact. To be safe, they seldom offer an
opinion, even when asked; if they do reply, frequently it is to echo
the opinion of someone else. In one-on-one conversations, they
become experts at asking questions, keeping the focus on the
other person, avoiding the spotlight where they will look unpol-
ished and foolish. Quiet Reactors are great spectators but infre-
quent players, unless the activity is one they excel at or at least
perform better than most. They do not allow others to really get
to know them because they don't reveal themselves.

Quiet Reactors with low self-esteem frequently practice being
invisible. They fear being seen in an adverse light and so act in
ways that will not bring attention to themselves, attention that
they surmise will be negative.

Here are ways those of us with LSE may practice being invisible:

- Dressing in subdued colors—blacks, browns, blues, dark or
  neutral colors

- Dressing very conservatively—avoiding trendy clothes or new
  styles.

- Sitting off to the side or in the back when we attend group functions.

- Being careful not to state an idea or opinion that might be controversial.

- Refusing to take part in any activity where we might look inadequate, especially a new activity at which we do not feel accomplished.

- Avoiding eye contact.

- Only attending social functions where we have a role to play that will keep us occupied, so that we have limited interaction with others.

- Asking questions of others to keep the focus off ourselves.

- Revealing little about our feelings, desires, dreams, ideas—information that reveals who we really are.

- Deferring to the wishes of others.

- Being overly agreeable.

- Avoiding the "limelight" in every way possible.

- Waiting for others to initiate, which may never happen.

- Talking so quietly in groups that we are not heard or are barely heard.

- Being unwilling to say what we want.

- Laughing a lot in place of talking.

Putting on the face of an attentive listener, a Quiet Reactor has difficulty fully concentrating. He is so busy thinking how he should respond, he may hear very little of what is being said to him. Needing to make conversation can be very anxiety-provoking. To avoid this, he may take on the role of helper where he can avoid interaction by being the person who refills the drinks, cleans up after the function, or watches the children. Even being the host or hostess can keep a person busy simply greeting people and overseeing the evening, so that he does not have to engage in conversation beyond greetings or light chatter. Basically, those who want to be invisible can find any number of tasks to do that remove them from the main activity and thereby from scrutiny.

All of these are, of course, self-defeating behaviors. They are temporary measures that may provide safety but that do nothing to remedy the problem or promote the desired interaction and closeness with others. Wanting to be involved in these opportunities to interact with others in order to gain confidence and develop socially, Quiet Reactors attend but then "hide" behind chosen responsibilities.

In addition, this constant effort to look and act like everyone else, to fit in and mirror others, merely serves to further obliterate the uniqueness of those with LSE; instead, they look as if they have nothing of interest to offer. By restricting their opportunities to express their specialness, they also limit the likelihood that someone will admire or recognize that uniqueness because it is not discernible. This is the ultimate self-sabotage, for what those with LSE want most is to connect emotionally with other people, yet their behavior denies them that possibility. Quiet Reactors have made passivity an art. They have perfected it. They live by it. Thus, assertiveness training and developing a thorough understanding of what it means to be assertive is essential (see Chapter 9).

Another negative consequence experienced by Quiet Reactors occurs when they cannot respond in the middle of a conflict. Deeply upset or frozen with fear, people with LSE are often unable to defend themselves or express their emotions. This silence, interpreted inaccurately as "the silent treatment," elicits the wrath of others who think they are being deliberately punished.

- *A note of comparison with those with healthy self-esteem:*

People with healthy self-esteem are neither Noisy nor Quiet Reactors. This does not mean that people with healthy self-esteem are never boisterous, obnoxious, or quiet in responding, nor does it mean that they are always assertive. Instead, they may be motivated by differing standards or have other disorders that make them disruptive or overbearing. They may be passive for other reasons other than low self-esteem, such as not caring enough to speak up about something, or being too lazy to assert themselves. Most people with healthy self-esteem, however enjoy communicating and are skilled at appropriate interacting. They are generally socially appropriate and are aware of how their behavior impacts others.

RECOVERY

People with LSE can alter their self-defeating behaviors. They can learn to have healthy, honest relationships; they can obtain the social skills that they are lacking and learn to act in more appropriate ways. Most people with LSE are not aware that they sabotage themselves or that they destroy their own relationships. They tend not to be introspective or at least not in a way that produces the desired effects. Their attempts at self-analysis are geared more toward self-criticism or self-justification. They have difficulty moving beyond their emotions to actually making changes. This, of course, needs to be the focus. The purpose of this book is to help you become aware, not so that you will feel even worse about yourself, but so that you can begin to take the steps toward recovery.

THINGS TO DO

Exercise 1

Most people who perform self-defeating behaviors are not fully aware that they do. They are so focused on not embarrassing themselves and avoiding threatening situations that they do not see the big picture—the overall patterns that result in lasting negative effects on their lives. This exercise will help you become more aware of the specific things you do that sabotage your life.

1. Think of ways you have sabotaged yourself with self-defeating behaviors. List these in your notebook. Be specific. (Refer to the list on pages 103-104 if needed.)

2. One by one, describe in writing what you think were the results of those situations in which you sabotaged yourself.

3. How could you have acted differently, so as not to sabotage yourself? Again, be specific. Write this down. (If you cannot come up with possible alternatives, discuss this with a close friend or your therapist. Be open to suggestions.)

4. Picture what might have happened if you had acted differently. What might you have done? Try to be positive. Add this to your notebook.

5. Pick one of the situations from No. 1. Follow its sequence through each answer you have given. Picture yourself responding differently. Again, I encourage you to remain positive.

6. Try to imagine how your life might be different if you had not performed that one self-sabotage. Try to see how your choices in the future can impact your life.

7. Choose one self-defeating behavior you regularly do. (Choose a small one.) Think how you can do this differently the next opportunity you have. Make a commitment to yourself to try a new behavior the next time.

8. Whenever you are able to successfully replace an old self-defeating behavior with a new one, write a description of your success in your notebook and reward yourself in some way— an ice-cream cone, a new magazine, extra time for yourself, a bicycle ride, or whatever would be, for you, a pat on the back.

THINGS TO DO

Exercise 2

This exercise is another attempt to help us to understand how we operate in the world, and to help us to know ourselves better. As we become aware of how and why we act as we do, we can better recognize our self-defeating patterns; we will then be more equipped to work toward change. Try this exercise.

1. Reread the sections on Noisy and Quiet Reactors to refresh your memory.

2. Think back to your own past behaviors. Are you usually a Quiet Reactor? A Noisy Reactor?

3. List the specific behaviors that you have performed as either a Noisy or Quiet Reactor. What exactly did you do?

4. Think of ways you could become a healthy actor, possibly replacing a self-defeating behavior that you now habitually perform with a more moderate reaction.

5. Picture how the situation would look if you acted differently. Imagine how it would feel. Remain positive.

6. Determine to change one small aspect of how you now respond. Choose a specific goal.

5

Learning to be Alone

JANE: how the past shapes her fears

Growing up, Jane felt insecure and distraught. She had developed a good relationship with her father, but her mother remained critical and disapproving. Rigid in her expectations of others, Jane's mother seemed especially hostile when Jane's ideas or behavior did not mirror her own. For example, Jane was by nature a night person and an introvert. She was unable to go to sleep very early and enjoyed the late evening hours when everyone else was in bed; she loved quiet time when she could read or do projects in her bedroom. Her mother believed that everyone should go to bed early and arise early; she and Jane had struggled continually with this difference of opinion. She would even tell others how lazy her daughter was even though Jane pointed out that she slept no longer than anyone else in the family, just during different hours.

During these years, Jane felt very much alone. Her mother did not appreciate Jane's differences and frequently told her so. Jane felt no one understood her; she had no one to talk to. She often cried herself to sleep at night, feeling frightened and very sad.

Though Jane is surrounded by her immediate family, she often feels alone and misunderstood. Later in life, this absence of support and approval causes her to feel desperate for a relationship; when she develops one, she tries to hang on to it tightly, because she fears returning to being alone.

The Experience of Being Alone

Spending time alone is uncomfortable for many people, especially those with LSE, who find it difficult to enjoy their own company. Being uncoupled (without a significant other) is even more agonizing because it means that the person is totally responsible for himself and for filling his time. He has no one with whom to share decisions, work, or other obligations.

Being single, living alone, and being without a significant other are not all that unusual today. Fewer people are choosing to marry, though they may have a significant other. Many are alone, not by choice but because they have not found someone with whom they want to share their lives. Some are alone because they have not developed the skills necessary to establish a lasting relationship; others are alone following a failed relationship. Some, though coupled, still feel alone because they lack a real relationship with their mates or those around them.

Of those who are single, some are content while others are unhappy and lonely. Many who have experienced dysfunctional or abusive relationships find living alone quite satisfactory. Introverted individuals who thrive on peace and quiet may especially find living alone and large amounts of alone time appealing. Others feel negatively labeled when they do not have a significant other in their lives; they think the world is geared to couples and they feel self-conscious going places unaccompanied.

Those who believe being alone invalidates their worth find singleness a difficult road to travel. They project this belief onto others and assume that people who know them are wondering why they are unattached. They may feel out of place when they're with couples or families. It is understandable that singles may feel inferior when we live in a society where "family values" is a popular term, where those invited are expected to bring a "date," where discounts are often given to couples, and where married couples receive tax, retirement, and other benefits unavailable to singles. In addition, older women who have never married are still often labeled "old maids," and many people still equate singleness with immaturity or inadequacy.

We also live in a society in which women are obsessed with analyzing relationships. On television talk shows, in magazines and books of all kinds, women especially seem to thrive on stories of success and failure in relationships. Consequently, articles and books abound on how to improve one's sex life, how to find a mate, how to win and keep a man. For many women, unfortunately, being in a relationship is the goal of their lives.

To the person alone, this persistent focus on relationship can add up to considerable pressure. A woman may question herself, wondering why she hasn't succeeded in finding a mate; she may enter therapy to find the cause or, like Jane, even accept a relationship that is unhealthy. If she has low self-esteem and is already questioning her worth and adequacy, she will tend to experience even more self-doubt. Since the media encourages her to believe that anyone can have a relationship if only she uses the right perfume, wears the right panty hose, drinks the right soda, or chews the right breath mints, being alone screams "failure."

Advertising tells men that they should focus on the appearance of women to find a partner. Long blonde hair flowing in the wind, long legs, sexy clothes, and sparkling teeth are what to look for. Substance is not even a consideration but is absurdly assumed to come along with the package. Ads also indicate that the good-smelling cologne or the purchase of a new sports car or macho truck will likely attract a partner. This type of thinking doesn't help anyone, let alone the person with LSE, to find a suitable mate. And, while most men may not focus on the relationship in the analytical way women do, they too want to have the satisfaction and contentment that comes from having a compatible mate or companion.

"Smile the right way, look the right way, and own the right things, and you will find the right person." This message is powerful and convincing—almost everyone wants a significant other— and as a society, people spend millions responding to the bait.

The problems with this way of thinking, however, are many:

- Being in a relationship does not guarantee being loved or even respected.

- Being in a relationship does not guarantee happiness.

- Being in a relationship may not promote independence, personal growth, or healthy self-esteem.

- Being in a relationship is not by itself an indication of adequacy or competency.

- Being in a relationship should complement an already fully developed life; it should not be the goal.

- Being in a bad relationship or being in a relationship for the wrong reasons can be both physically and mentally destructive.

- Being in a bad relationship often results in a person losing a sense of self.

Being in a relationship can enhance a person's life or decrease the quality of her existence. For example, a relationship that encourages both partners to grow intellectually and emotionally can be very rewarding; a relationship that offers support for ideas and opinions can motivate and energize. And when a relationship includes mutual respect, it increases the depth of intimacy. (For more on intimacy in relationships, see: *Low Self-Esteem in the Bedroom: How LSE affects Intimacy*, Sorensen, Wolf, 2004.) A good relationship can provide companionship, support and encouragement, a partner in decision-making, someone with whom to share the work of maintaining a home, and financial stability. Such a relationship can bring joy to a person's life.

On the other hand, being single is an ideal situation for some people at certain points in their lives. When people are troubled, undecided about direction in their lives or grieving losses, they are not in a position to focus on a relationship; they are confused and their energy resources are depleted. When people are unsure of who they are, when they have personal work that needs to be done, they are unable to be an equal partner in a relationship; they are too needy. If they are not already in a relationship, these people should first attend to their own business of personal development and healing. Unfortunately, it is often at those periods that people, especially those with LSE, look for someone whose attention will make them feel better—a quick fix that provides temporary relief but that does nothing to solve their real problems. In addition, their sense of desperation may lead them to enter into relationships that may not be what they really need, even though these relationships provide immediate gratification.

Thus, the choice to be single or partnered should be based on a person's real needs, as well as on the merits of the people available to meet some of those needs. The truth: Being in a relationship is not a measure of a person's worth but is more an indication of a person's choices, whether good or bad. Nearly everyone could be in a relationship if they are willing to compromise their standards and tolerate abuse, neglect, and immaturity. Finding a *suitable* partner is the more difficult task.

Being Alone: The Real Issues for Those with LSE

The inability to be alone indicates unresolved issues or lack of development in crucial areas of our lives. We may need to learn to face our inner selves, develop personal interests, overcome our guilt about doing for ourselves, or learn to be more independent.

1. Facing the inner self

Being alone, whether because we are single or because we have periods of free time, forces us to confront ourselves, to look at who we are, at how far we have come and from where, at what we want and need in life, and at how we plan to attain that. Uncertain of our self-worth, we may not enjoy our own company; we may be anxious about looking at those personal issues. Additionally, we may find that having quiet time alone forces us to confront our demons—troublesome memories from our past and the lingering feelings that accompany them.

Staying busy or continually requiring the company of others, on the other hand, allows us to ignore our fears by displacing our anxiety. By focusing on something else, we can temporarily divert the anxiety and push the fear away; when we are alone again, however, we are soon aware that the fear and anxieties are not gone but have only been temporarily repressed.

Personal emotional growth requires that we be willing to look at and evaluate ourselves, after which we can take steps to further improve those qualities we find undeveloped. For example, we may need to ask ourselves why we haven't gotten further in our careers and find that we need to get more training; we may realize that we are not happy in our present job and then decide to pursue something else. We may realize that we haven't given ourselves the opportunity to develop personal interests and decide to take classes in photography or carpentry; we may face the fact that we have been irresponsible with our finances and take steps to change this. In other words, we need to face our own problems and take positive steps to correct them.

Being in a relationship can at times require and at other times lure us to focus our energy on other people and their goals and, in so doing, impede our ability to stay centered on finding ourselves and discovering our personal mission in life. In other words, being in a relationship can be a substitute for dealing with our own challenges. We can put our energy into the relationship and ignore our own issues.

2. Developing personal interests

If we have healthy self-esteem, we look forward to time alone when we can pursue our interests, hobbies, and activities. LSE, however, causes us to be fearful of expressing our creativity, to be insecure about facing new challenges, and to be anxious about making decisions. We may have devoted ourselves to endeavors in which we felt comfortable, like our work or family responsibilities, while rationalizing that we didn't have time for ourselves. Now when we do have time, we don't know how to use it.

We may not have had practice at actually planning ahead to have the supplies we need to enjoy time alone, like flower seeds to plant or books to read. We may not know how to get organized, so that when we do have time for ourselves, we don't know where to begin. Consequently, we feel anxious and uncertain about how to proceed. Unfamiliar with the joy that accompanies involvement in hobbies and interests, we view the required effort or planning as more trouble than they're worth. Only when we venture forth, develop an interest, and get totally submerged in that interest can we experience the payoff; we learn that the enjoyment then usually far outweighs the work and energy first required.

Having spent our lives avoiding new adventures or denying ourselves opportunities to develop our talents or pursue our interests, we may not have found anything fascinating or stimulating to fill our time. Most people with LSE are virtually unaware of their feelings and emotions other than fear and anxiety; this means they are unaware of what they like and dislike. Ask someone with LSE what she would like to do if she had a full day for any activity and she may say that she has no idea other than her daily responsibilities or routine. Ask many people who have low self-esteem what specific things they want to accomplish in their lifetime, what places they want to visit, or what dreams they have and they may say, "I don't know. I've never thought about it." Tending to live in the present—just trying to cope—they may not be able to envision the future or feel there is much point in having dreams. People with LSE have spent their time attempting to allay their fears and quiet their anxieties through avoidance, isolation, and pleasing others. Many have basically lost themselves.

When we do get involved in personal interests, our efforts often lead to involvement with other people. Those we meet who share similar interests may later become our friends; they may someday make up our support group. With an interest in common, we are freer to interact around that mutual enjoyment in a more natural way, without the pressure that accompanies pursuit of a romantic relationship.

3.   Overcoming guilt

Being accustomed to pleasing others, we may feel guilty setting aside time for ourselves or for our own activities. We may be so geared to meeting the needs of others that it is foreign to us to think of meeting our own or going after the things we want. When forced to think about such things, we may feel that it is selfish to focus solely on ourselves and our desires. We may not be aware that our first responsibility is actually to value and develop ourselves. Those who try to please others while remaining miserable themselves tend to smother others, give for the wrong reasons, and

end up pleasing no one. As singles, we should buy fresh flowers to enjoy (though no company is expected), take time to enjoy a leisurely bubble bath (though we have no plans to go out), spend money purchasing something special that we've always wanted (it doesn't have to be expensive), or fix our favorite desserts—just for us. We might buy tickets to that athletic event and even buy the best seat possible; we might
spend the money on that new jacket or software game we want. We might take a day and drive to the beach or have that tummy tuck done just because we want to do so.

4. Becoming independent

We may have difficulty being alone because in the past we have not taken charge of our own lives. Instead, we may have knowingly and willingly relied on others to provide a sense of meaning for our existence. We may have been in a relationship where someone else took control and did not allow us the freedom to choose for ourselves or make normal decisions. These partners were more like parents than equals, or perhaps they were domineering and abusive. Having LSE, we may have participated in this form of confinement by remaining in the situation. Battered and bruised (emotionally and/or physically), we may now be too anxious to know how to regain control of our lives and make constructive decisions. We may have been chastised by these controlling people for considering our own needs and now feel anxious and guilty taking time for ourselves, so that we only focus on what we "should" do for others. When we have long been dependent on others for direction in our lives, becoming an independent person is difficult and takes time.

The necessity of learning to be alone

When alone, we can slow down both physically and emotionally; our minds become less cluttered with mundane details, allowing underlying, painful feelings and memories to rise to the surface. This is a frightening process, however, because those of us who have LSE don't know what to do with the hurtful memories, feelings of betrayal, and reminders of past losses that come to mind during these periods of solitude and silence. As we avoid looking at our inner selves, we forestall the healing process by denying ourselves the opportunity to know what we really feel, fear, and desire.

Facing and overcoming our fears about being alone is a first step to feeling adequate, competent, and worthy. While alone, we can look at our issues without distractions; we can concentrate on sorting out, understanding, and recovering from the past. This process can extricate us from our guilt and enable us to see ourselves as unique and worthwhile individuals. Time alone provides us with the opportunity to better understand who we are, how we feel, and what we want in life; we can become more stable individuals, people who are more mature and less needy. As we then develop new skills and set appropriate goals, we can become more independent, people who are free to be ourselves and who can plan for a better future.

Being alone presents all of us with the opportunity to attend to our needs, to become acquainted with those things we enjoy, to make our own decisions, to listen to our inner voice, to develop our choice-making processes, and to appreciate who we are. Being uncoupled allows time to discover the things we value and allows time to learn to be present with ourselves in peace. When we understand the benefits of "alone" time and view singleness as an opportunity for self-development, it can be a period in our life of significant growth rather than an interval we view as symbolic of our inadequacy. This time alone may be the ideal period to commit yourself to therapy and the process of recovery from low self-esteem.

While the author is not suggesting that you end a relationship in order to recover from low self-esteem, learning to be alone can be an important step in the self-esteem recovery process. Being alone can also be a frightening experience in the beginning. Those who have fought this fear report that the actual process, while painful, proved to alter the course of their entire lives. Many, in retrospect, see it was a turning point, a time when they faced their low self-esteem and determined to overcome it.

One of the keys to enjoying time alone is learning to like ourselves. The following are necessary components:

- We must learn to take pleasure in our own presence, secure in the fact that:

    1. We can comfortably experience our own thoughts and feelings.

    2. We are fully capable of handling our affairs.

    3. We can use this time to plan, to examine, to enjoy the small things in life, to grow and expand our interests and hobbies.

- We must learn to respect ourselves, including our character, our standards, and our beliefs:

    1. By examining our values and standards, evaluating them, and readjusting them if necessary.

    2. By thinking about the how we act, live, and treat others as well as the way in which others probably view us, then analyzing whether we are being who we want to be.

3. By setting goals for change in the areas we feel lacking or off-balance in our lives.

• We must learn to admire ourselves as we achieve our goals, form our opinions, work through our ideas, and express our creativity.

1. We may need to expand our scope of information.

2. We may want to find ways to learn about interests we've never pursued.

3. We may need to find an organization or group in which to exchange ideas and thereby stimulate our thinking.

• We must each come to the place where we recognize our uniqueness.

1. We may need to develop our individuality through interests that make us unique and, therefore, more interesting.

2. We may need to take the risk of taking lessons to become more skilled at something.

3. We may need to find ways to help others, to excel at something, to do something we've always wanted to do but never had the courage to try. Only as we take risks, gain knowledge, or develop our skills can we recognize our uniqueness.

Learning to value ourselves

To accomplish this goal of respecting ourselves and being at peace with ourselves, we need to exert ourselves in learning whatever we need to so that we will feel secure in making decisions. We might take a class on finances so we can better handle our money or get career counseling to become more aware of our talents and available opportunities. We might begin reading the newspaper to become better informed, get involved in a community project to feel we are doing our part, join a health club or a garden club, begin individual counseling, read books, or join a political organization. We might consider learning to meditate, taking a class on yoga, joining a book club, beginning an exercise program, or learning to backpack. These endeavors will broaden our view of life, assist us in deciding what we believe and what we stand for, enable us to get to know and appreciate ourselves, and ultimately build self-respect. We will be developing ourselves, through our own efforts, as a result of our own choices, and we will reap the benefits.

While this is a long process, we can make the journey and we can reach the destination, though we may need assistance along the way. Because we are so ingrained in our dysfunctional patterns, we may not be able, at first, to spot those patterns or know what and how to do anything differently. Therapy may be necessary; we may need an objective person to direct us as we start down this new road; later, we can take the wheel ourselves.

• *A note of comparison with those with healthy self-esteem:*

Healthy people treasure time alone, when they are free to use their minds and their creativity. Because they feel good about themselves, they enjoy the opportunity to think, to ponder, to plan, to rest, to clarify, all without the need to have anyone present. They have worked through their grief from the past and are basically free from the guilt that often accompanies unresolved issues. They are independent; they have goals and dreams for the future.

Healthy individuals do not become desperate or depressed whenever they are without a significant other; instead, they enter into healthy friendships and choose to be alone when they do not have a potentially healthy candidate for a partner. They do not feel as though they are inadequate when they are alone.

Happy, energetic, and involved when single, healthy people do not view singleness as a sign of unworthiness. They seek to be in a significant relationship not out of a "need" to feel adequate, but because they desire to share their lives with another person who they believe will enhance their already fulfilling life. They believe that it is better to be single than partnered with an unhealthy individual.

Extroversion & Introversion

To understand the different ways in which people with LSE respond to their anxiety about being uncoupled or spending time alone, it is important to understand the difference between introversion and extroversion. The common but inaccurate belief is that introverts are people who are inappropriately shy—maybe even anti-social—a problem they need to overcome, while extroverts are outgoing, the acceptable way to operate in the world. In fact, it is not that introverts are shy, but rather that they are reserved and quiet whereas extroverts are demonstrative and talkative. Neither behavior pattern is better than the other; they are merely different.

The following explains the actual differences between introverts and extroverts.

- *Extroverts* organize their thoughts as they speak—they do not need time to process internally. They throw out ideas that are only in the formation stage or thoughts that pop into their heads without having first been fully digested. They tend to say whatever they are thinking. They tend to formulate their opinions as they talk.[1]

  Introverts need to think things through quietly in their heads before sharing their opinions or thoughts; by the time they voice their ideas and opinions, they have given thorough thought to their position.

- *Extroverts* are stimulated by their external environment; they are energized by being with people, attending a concert, or talking on the phone—anything that provides variety and action. They are enthusiastic but get bored easily when they are inactive. When extroverts become discouraged or depressed, they generally need to be active and with other people.

  Introverts are energized by their own thinking—their inner world of ideas and thoughts; consequently, they require time alone to ponder, to analyze, to evaluate. They enjoy working alone and dislike telephone interruptions. When introverts become discouraged or overwhelmed, they generally need time alone.

- *Extroverts* enjoy large groups and group activities, the more the merrier; they love parties. Many talk fast and dominate conversations. They are skilled at and enjoy talking superficially with others, even new acquaintances, about a great number of topics.

[1] Kroeger, Oto and Janet M. Thusen. *Type Talk*. Delacorte Press: New York, 1998, pp. 13-16.

Introverts are generally quite intense and prefer to spend time in small groups or one on one; they are often uncomfortable in large group settings. Generally good listeners, they prefer to talk in depth to people they know well and may not be good at chitchat. They are very talkative when addressing an issue about which they are very interested or well informed. While not shy, they are reflective and reserved.

• Both extroverts and introverts can have low self-esteem.

Understanding the distinctions between extroverts and introverts can be extremely helpful to us. Recognizing these differences can help those in relationships to understand one another, whether friends or partners, boss and employee, or parent and child. Realizing how extroverts and introverts think and behave differently increases our sensitivity to the needs of others and may explain why people act in the ways they do. For example, this knowledge might explain the reluctance of a spouse to attend frequent office functions, large concerts, or family gatherings—behavior that we may have interpreted as unsupportive, uncaring, or unloving.

Extroverts and LSE

The idea of allotting time to be alone is foreign to many extroverts, who spend their lives darting from one activity to the next. They thrive on being busy; they love constant stimulation and interaction. Too much time alone can be depressing for them. This is even more true of extroverts who have LSE: They cannot deal with silence or inactivity and may become frantic when alone. They have difficulty being without a significant other; instead they long for someone to interact with so they will not have to be alone. Consequently, extroverts with low self-esteem frequently form relationships in which they and their partners are inseparable, often totally enmeshed; their insecurity combined with their extroversion produces a desperate fear of being alone. They feel equally uncomfortable when their partners are with others, feeling left out and unimportant.

Extroverts can exhaust others, especially introverts, with their chatter, their never-ending plans, and their many activities. Extroverts with LSE who are uncoupled often "wear out" their friends by constantly demanding attention and companionship. Those with LSE who are not single often have tumultuous relationships because they are likely to verbalize all of their wants, needs, and grievances while not listening well to their partners. Because of the neediness that accompanies LSE, they may provoke constant dramas that need to be discussed and solved; they can consume the lives of others if allowed to do so.

Extroverts especially need to learn to spend time alone. Rather than merely filling their time with activities and meetings, they need to focus on their own development. These extroverts need to realize that external stimulation cannot heal the internal wounds caused by their LSE—that a relationship cannot serve as the balm that will cure and restore.

Introverts and LSE

Introverts by nature keep to themselves much more than extroverts; however, those with LSE isolate even more. When plagued by their self-esteem issues, they may call a friend but only if it is someone they trust completely. Generally they stay home, needing long periods of time to process their thoughts; they do not readily initiate with others and have fewer friends than extroverts. (Even introverts with healthy self-esteem do not have the large number of friends that extroverts do; more inclined to intense discussion than extroverts and less skilled at chitchat, they choose, instead, to develop a few quality relationships.)

Because introverts are in the minority in our society, being introverted contributes to the low self-esteem of many adults; as children, they may have been criticized for not being like others more gregarious than they. Like introverted adults, introverted children like to be alone and play alone. They often avoid group activities and enjoy doing things that require that they think. They can often be found reading or doing activities that do not require the presence of others. Seeing their child alone much of the time, parents often become concerned and try to push him to interact more with others, join groups, or attend school functions. These parents are unaware that such situations are unpleasant for the child because he is introverted; they misinterpret his behavior as some form of maladjustment. Throughout their lives, introverts frequently hear people saying to them, "Why don't you want to go outside and play with the other kids (attend the school dance, go to the party, join the team, etc.) like everyone else?" The message the introvert hears is that there is something wrong with her. Those with LSE take this even more to heart; already feeling inadequate, their low opinions of themselves are cemented by these remarks.

Healthy introverts naturally and consciously attempt to spend sufficient amounts of time alone; they have less need of relationships, though they may desire one with the right person. Introverts with LSE, however, may seek relationships to ease their pain and loneliness, viewing a relationship as proof of their worthiness, yet once in a relationship, they may be non-communicative because their introversion and self-esteem issues steer them to protect their inner feelings.

People with LSE feel nervous and are unable to relax when they are alone. Frequently bored anyway, extroverts especially feel the need to be constantly doing something: watching television, talking on the phone, playing with their computer; keeping busy, they do not want to "think" about themselves or their lives. Introverts with LSE internalize, spending hours ruminating over their feelings of inadequacy, often plunging into depression.

Extroverts generally say that they spend ample time alone; those with LSE, however, avoid using this time for reflection or self-analysis, tending instead to stay busy with various distractions. Extroverts prefer to surround themselves with people. They can, however, be so focused on what they want to say that they fail to hear what others are saying. Extroverts with LSE may be especially poor listeners because they are so self-focused. Wanting to speak but too fearful to reveal their deeper feelings, they may spend their time in group activities in which their true selves can remain hidden; thus they remain safe, but deny themselves the opportunity to form the close relationships they desire.

Introverts with LSE, on the other hand, may choose to be alone in order to isolate or hide while dealing with depression, humiliation, or despair. They lack the motivation, energy, resources, or courage to be with others as they are unable to internally resolve their problems or do anything constructive about them.

It is important that we do not confuse introvert with Quiet Reactors or think the terms extrovert and Noisy Reactor are identical. Noisy and Quiet Reactors specifically identify the contrasting styles in which those with LSE react when in conflict; an extrovert can be either a Noisy or Quiet Reactor just as an introvert can be either. For example, an introvert with LSE, who needs time to reflect and analyze a negative situation (typical of introverts), may isolate at first; later in anger, she becomes a Noisy Reactor when she actually responds to another person. In the same situation, an extrovert may immediately respond (typical of extroverts), figuring out his position as he talks, but do so hesitantly and quietly, uncertain if what he is saying is accurate .

An introvert may react in a quiet fashion most of the time and then become a Noisy Reactor when she can no longer hold in her rage or when someone behaves in ways that are similar to past abuse she has endured, triggering this explosive reaction. An extrovert who has no support system may tell his problems to complete strangers, defusing his anger; he may then respond to the actual situation quietly.

Extroverts are adept at talking about most topics; introverts can talk incessantly if you engage them in a conversation about something they have previously thought through, including areas in which they are particularly knowledgeable or interested. Either may do this in a noisy or quiet manner.

• *A note of comparison with those with healthy self-esteem:*

Healthy people do not have difficulty listing their good qualities; they are very aware of the things they do well and are mindful of their past accomplishments. They are independent and do not rely on others to make their decisions, although they readily seek advice. Healthy introverts and extroverts enjoy activities that require no interaction with others but themselves and their environment alone. Both enjoy the company of others, although extroverts seem to need more frequent interaction and more group activities. They can both be quiet; they can allow their senses to direct their time alone.

Being alone vs. being lonely

Loneliness has little to do with whether a person is coupled or single. Many people who are married or coupled are still lonely, while many single people are not. Instead, people feel lonely when they lack emotional connections with others. For example, a single person may have one or more good friends whom she talks to and spends time with who are understanding and concerned, who like her and are interested in her well-being. While not in a committed romantic relationship with any of these people, she may feel supported, cared about, and connected; she may feel content.

Another person may be in a committed relationship with a partner but not feel emotionally close, truly supported, or even respected by that partner. If this person does not have others in her life who provide for these needs, she experiences a sense of loneliness even though she is coupled. Thus, it is not the coupled state of the person that guarantees the absence of loneliness, but rather the presence of a close, emotionally supportive, and trustworthy person in one's life.

There are five levels on which all people can communicate with others: the surface level, the factual level, the thinking level, the feeling level, and the intimacy level. Learning first to like ourselves, learning second how to communicate on all of these levels, and learning third to find trustworthy, caring people with whom to communicate are the steps to overcoming loneliness. All three of these elements are necessary; the key to feeling content rather than feeling lonely, however, lies in our ability to develop and maintain a relationship in which we can communicate at the two deepest levels of communication, the feeling and intimacy levels.

The following describes levels of communication and emotional closeness:

- **The Surface Level**—At level 1, the simplest form of communication occurs. We talk in clichés or superficially about general topics, e.g., "How's it going?" "Nice day, isn't it?" At this level, we can talk without knowing anything about the other person and without revealing anything about ourselves. It is totally safe. We might make such comments to a neighbor, to a gas station attendant, or to our postal delivery person. No relationship has been established although we may see this person frequently. (Extroverts are good at this. Introverts are less likely to initiate this type of interaction.)

- **The Factual Level**—More involvement occurs at the factual level as we share facts about situations or happenings we know about or have experienced. Such comments as "Aunt Hazel is in the hospital," "I'm getting a promotion at work," "We went to Disneyland this summer," or "I've been having trouble with my car" are all examples of conversing at level 2. This is also a form of safe communication because facts leave no room for debate or disagreement; we are merely sharing indisputable facts. (Once again, extroverts do this readily; introverts find this level of communication less enjoyable.)

- **The Thinking Level**—When communicating on level 3, we share our opinions, ideas, and perceptions about the world, about ourselves and about our personal lives. This a deeper level of interacting and one that is more threatening because such responses can be challenged. To talk freely at this level, we must have confidence in ourselves and our conclusions; lacking that confidence, we will be reluctant to share our thinking, knowing others might disagree or even take offense at our remarks. We must trust the other person—that they will respect our opinions, ideas, and perceptions whether or not they agree. Only when two people both feel comfortable sharing at this level with one another and actively do so, do they have a "level 3 relationship." Developing such a trust level with another person takes time. When we are around a person in a variety of situations and over a period of time, we are able to discern if the person is trustworthy; only then will we feel comfortable talking on this level about our opinions and our ideas. (Introverts thrive on talking at this level about topics on which they are well versed, though those with LSE will be less inclined to do so. Extroverts enjoy this level of discussion whether or not they are knowledgeable about the subject matter, though those with LSE may hold back their ideas and opinions out of fear.)

- **The Feeling Level**—This type of communicating requires that we reveal who we really are, how we truly feel about ourselves, about our dreams and our disappointments; at this level, intimacy is developing as we experience increasing vulnerability by opening our inner selves up to be viewed by our listener. In order to truly communicate at level 4, we must feel "safe" with the person we are speaking to; we must feel accepted, respected, and free from threatening repercussions. Sharing at this level is the beginning, the key to developing true intimacy, while the inability to share at this level prevents intimacy from occurring. Only when both individuals feel comfortable sharing at this level with one another does a "level 4 relationship" exist. (Both extroverts and introverts enjoy talking at this level. Those with LSE, however, may feel too vulnerable to honestly share their feelings with another person; they may not even be aware of how they feel.)

- **The Intimacy Level**—At this level, we are able to share our deepest feelings, concerns, most embarrassing moments, and pain without any fear of reprisal; we feel fully accepted and loved by the other. We can talk about positive happenings without anticipation that we will be judged as boasting. We can share our shortcomings and our humiliation without fear that it will alter the other person's feelings about us. We are free to say whatever is on our minds, knowing we will continue to be loved and accepted. This level of communication can only be achieved through a growing and abiding trust that has developed over time between two mature individuals. A "level 5 relationship" requires reciprocity; it is difficult to achieve and requires tender loving care to maintain. Few people ever achieve such a relationship in their lifetime, probably because most people are unwilling to devote the time and energy necessary to develop and maintain such a deep relationship. In addition, those with LSE may lack the self-assurance to be able to reveal themselves to the extent required for such a relationship, or having never experienced this type of emotional connection with another person, they don't recognize the intrinsic value or even the existence of this level of communication.

People who presently have a true and reciprocal level 4 or 5 relationship do not feel lonely, though they may have experienced loneliness in the past and may again in the future. This deep connection occurs in both same or opposite-sex friendships or romantic relationships. Unfortunately, this level of interacting occurs more often between women than between men and women or between men because women in general place a higher priority on developing and maintaining verbal and emotional intimacy than men do.

As a result, the majority of people in committed, physically-intimate relationships do not experience emotional intimacy and do not have level 4 or 5 relationships. They may occasionally share feelings but feel uncomfortable doing so; they may not share their feelings at all. One of the couple may share on that level while the other does not. Women in relationships with men often do not even share at a level 3 with their partner because these women do not feel their opinions, ideas, and perceptions are valued.

People with LSE have difficulty forming intimate relationships because they feel too inhibited and insecure to share even at level 3. They are fearful of more rejection; they are fearful of being put down for their opinions and ideas. Obviously, when people are too frightened to let others see who they are, they will have difficulty forming close relationships, even though they desire to do so; they will be unable to dispel their feelings of loneliness.

The keys to a good relationship:

- Mutual respect for differences and feelings

- Mutual feelings of admiration, love, belonging, being part of a couple

- Mutual trust based on each having proved themselves to be trustworthy

- Similar values including those of integrity, loyalty, dependability, and principled choices

- A desire to be together based on *wanting* rather than *needing* to be with the other person

- A desire to support and encourage each other in good times and bad with careers, personal projects, individual interests, personal growth, and health issues

- Independent thinking and acting rather than codependent behavior

- A willingness by both people to address and work through problems

- The freedom to be ourselves, to make our own choices, to have our own thoughts, to draw our own conclusions, to have our own friends, to pursue our own interests, have control of our own money, have the right to decide how and when we expend our energy and our time

- A willingness to set aside adequate quality time for the relationship

- A willingness to work toward verbal, emotional, and physical intimacy

- A desire to be together, to spend time together

- A willingness to contribute time, energy, money, and skills to enhancing the relationship

- A willingness to share in the responsibilities and demands of a shared lifestyle

- A desire to meet the needs of the other partner to a healthy extent

Why Even Be in a Relationship?

Healthy relationships are ones in which both partners are healthy individuals or individuals striving to become more healthy and who have interests, goals, friends, activities, and a sense of worth not related to the partner. Just as a chain can be no stronger than its weakest link, so too a relationship can only be as healthy as its least healthy member. People who seek relationships to heal themselves or avoid their problems are incapable of fully completing their responsibilities to a healthy relationship; instead, they become either too dependent and compliant and devote all their energy to the other or they become too self-focused, demanding, and selfish in their expectations or they become self-focused, guarded, and withholding, frequently wounded by the words and actions of their partner. When one partner is not healthy, communication becomes strained, decision-making becomes more difficult, equality in the relationship cannot be achieved, and true intimacy is impossible.

Healthy relationships are formed when two healthy individuals decide that they would not only like to retain their personal interests and sense of self, but that they would also like to form an "us" with someone else and add a new entity to their lives. This is not a "giving up" of the individual—two do not become one— rather two become three as the chart below indicates. Thus, each person maintains individuality while agreeing to share a portion of their lives with the other.

Jane and John didn't have this kind of relationship; instead, they had one in which Jane was totally dependent on John, one in which Jane had given up her sense of self. This diagram indicates how the healthy relationship works; the discussion that follows describes what a healthy relationship would look like to Justin and Jamie if they decided to make a commitment to each other. This model applies to both heterosexual or same-sex relationships, in which each has individual freedoms, responsibility to the partner, and responsibility to the relationship.

In general, when an area of decision-making or conflict arises, the couple must again decide whether the concern is an "us" issue or an "individual" issue, and then to which partner the individual issue applies. If the issue is one that applies directly to one person and does not directly affect the other, the person it affects directly gets to make the final decision. If the concern affects both equally, a joint decision must be made. This may require extended discussion and consideration before the couple can arrive at a decision they both feel comfortable with, and that should be the goal. Any issue that falls, for example, in Jamie's column would be hers and hers alone to decide. She would likely solicit Justin's opinions or input, especially if her decision would have even minimal impact on him or the relationship, but the final decision would remain hers. In the same way, any issue in Justin's column would be his to resolve, though he would be wise to ask Jamie for her opinions and ideas about the issue. Thus, Jamie would have the right to decide who her friends would be, what personal goals she would have, and how she would spend her free time and money. She alone would have the right to decide how to dress, whom to vote for, and what career to choose. Justin, of course, would have the right to the same choices.

Example:

> *Elizabeth and Leon were in couple's counseling when Elizabeth began talking about how Leon wanted to spend nearly $800 to purchase a racing bike that she thought was unnecessary as he already had one. Leon defended his need for the bike. The psychologist asked how much discretionary money was available at the time. Leon said that they had nearly $2000 available and he only wanted to use 800 of it. The psychologist then suggested that maybe they could each take 800 and buy what they wanted. Elizabeth readily agreed, saying that would be fine with her. Leon, however objected, saying "Liz will just spend her money on jewelry." It then became clear, that Leon thought that his wants had more merit than Elizabeth's and that he wanted to be able to make the decisions for both of them; he saw his wants as justified and hers as frivolous. In the end, when Leon realized what he was doing, the two agreed to each take $800 and do whatever they wanted with it.*

Deciding where the choice lies can clearly illustrate where the responsibility falls and when one partner is into the other person's "stuff." For instance, how Jamie chooses to wear her hair, what interests she chooses to pursue, whether she is going to change jobs, or who her friends are are all individual choices. They are not "us" issues; they are not "us" choices. (Though changing jobs might require "us" consideration if it means a big difference in financial remuneration or relocating.) If Justin attempts to interfere with these decisions when they do not impact him negatively, he is in her "stuff." He has no right to dictate that she learn to play golf with him or attend his basketball games if she does not wish to do so, anymore than he must attend her softball games or read the same books she is interested in. She is not expected to be the cook on his hunting trips, or plan the menus, buy the groceries, set up the camp, and prepare the meals while he goes

Figure 3: Two Become Three

Two Become Three		
(Jamie)		(Justin)
Partner No. 1	Us	Partner No. 2
Individual friends	Shared friends	Individual friends
Individual goals	Shared goals	Individual goals
Individual interests	Shared interests	Individual interests
Financial goals	Shared financial goals	Financial goals
Control of personal expenditures	Division of financial resources	Control of personal expenditures
Career choices	Where to live	Career choices
Right to time alone	Time spent together	Right to time alone
Freedom to choose friends, how time is spent, dress, etc.	Shared errands	Freedom to choose friends, how time is spent, dress, etc.
Personal errands	Household responsibilities	Personal errands
	Shared life-style	
Right to initiate or decline sex with partner	Sexual relationship	Right to initiate or decline sex with partner
Right to personal beliefs and opinions		Right to personal beliefs and opinions
	Decision to have children	
	Shared parenting	

fishing. Both run their own errands or go to the store to pick up small needed items; both write letters and holiday cards to their own family and friends. Each participates in purchasing birthday gifts for family, friends, and siblings and wraps them. In a healthy relationship, the woman is not the "go-for," as was traditionally the case when women did not have careers or full-time jobs.

Within the "Us" column fall the choices that Jamie and Justin would make together because they had decided to share their lives. In a healthy relationship, they would consider together where they would live, whether they would rent or buy a home, if they would have children, how they would then divide childcare. For example, healthy couples both assume responsibility for their children. They might take turns bathing the children and putting them to bed. One might deliver them to school while the other picks them up at the end of the day. These couples do not assume that the woman is the primary caretaker while the man baby-sits occasionally. They work out their schedules regularly, determining who is responsible for childcare in the evenings, depending on the engagements each has. They both make arrangements for babysitters; they share childcare on the weekends and if both are home, they do not assume that the woman is in charge of the children. Both shop for their children's clothing, and both participate relatively equally in diaper changes, feeding, planning birthday parties, taking the children to their doctor appointments and parent-teacher consultations. Men in these relationships may take a week off to go fishing in Alaska, attend a meditation retreat or some conference, visit family, or go sailing with friends. Women in these relationships take similar amounts of time to attend a conference or retreat, go to the beach with a group of friends, photograph places in the Northeast in the fall, explore the covered bridges of Oregon, or backpack a leg of the Pacific Coast Trail. Each one takes care of the children and household responsibilities while the other is gone. Each one handles the arrangements for their trips. Both plan ahead, taking into consideration the schedule of the other and that of their children, discussing and agreeing on the timing of these times away.

Unlike in traditional relationships, where men usually take responsibility for the lawn, the cars, and dumping the garbage (chores that require irregular attention), the healthy male partner does not just "help out" within the home; the couple has worked together to fairly designate household chores. In fact, if both partners have full-time careers, all responsibilities are shared equally and the couple decides who does what, taking into consideration differing work schedules and work demands and preferably changing off from time to time so each is fully capable of completing all tasks should the need arise. Other choices that they make together include vacation choices, the amount and type of time spent together, and the nature and frequency of their sexual relationship. The couple works to make their sexual relationship mutually gratifying and neither is pressured to participate unwillingly.

If the couple determines that the subject of their conflict is an "us" issue, they must then come to some agreement on how to handle it. Frequently, healthy partners take turns making the decision if it is not a major one and they cannot easily agree. They may alternate choosing where to eat, what movie to attend, what activities they will participate in on the weekends. If, however, the issue clearly belongs to one partner, then the other must respect that person's right to make the decision without undue pressure.

Problems often occur when one or the other partner oversteps the boundaries and tries to force choices that are not his or hers to make. To pressure a partner to do what we want is a boundary violation, for no adult has the right to impose his/her wishes on another person. For example, if one partner has low self-esteem, that partner may feel threatened by independent decisions that the other partner makes that do not include her, even though she is not directly affected; if she then pressures the partner to change that decision, her attempt to change her partner's mind constitutes a boundary violation. A woman may decide to go back to school, spend a weekend at the beach with friends, take a class on assertiveness, or join a hiking club. Feeling insecure because she is expanding her world without him, her partner may attempt to sabotage her efforts by criticizing, by returning home late with the car so she cannot go, or by demanding her attention at times she has these commitments—also clear boundary violations. Feeling extremely vulnerable, the partner might attempt to reestablish a feeling of safety using drastic means such as threats, manipulation, or coercion, if necessary, because he equates security with control. Such situations arise frequently for those with LSE—both men and women; they are insecure and often equate independence in making choices with a lack of devotion to them and the relationship. For those with LSE, this behavior is common in other relationships as well, including those between siblings and close friends.

In a healthy relationship, both partners want the best for themselves and the best for the other person. They truly respect each other; they trust each other. They support and encourage each other, yet they maintain their own unique personalities and individuality. They do not try to control nor do they compete.

While, of course, this discussion is the tip of the iceberg when it comes to all the decisions a couple must make, it is nevertheless a beginning—a starting point or foundation from which to build, presenting the basic ideas for forming a healthy relationship. The model presented here not only allows for but also encourages independence, respect, equality, and personal responsibility. If followed, this plan prevents a couple from becoming mired down in codependency and enmeshment; it also provides a road map that enables the couple to discern when they are getting off track. Healthy men and women want to have such a relationship because it affords mutual respect. Some men, however, do not tolerate such a relationship because they see it as demanding far more of them than they have had to give in the past and more than they wish to contribute in the future. Most women, unless protecting their men or fearful they will be abandoned, clearly recognize that this type of relationship is fair to both and much healthier for both as well. Healthy, mature men usually agree.

Men and women often view relationships very differently. Women have generally been conditioned to put more emphasis on and, therefore, to be more focused on the quality of the relationship than men. Additionally, women have often experienced intimacy in their friendships with other women and seek to have a similar experience in a relationship with a significant other. Men in our society have always been awarded power and entitlement because they are male while that same culture continues to relegate women to a less important position. Many men are threatened by the idea of equal relationships because they actually view themselves as superior; they view a potential mate as a helpmate, sexual outlet, and companion—not as an equal. This is gradually changing, however, as men experience intimacy and quality relationships and want to both have and maintain them.

Society and the history of women

Societal views have contributed to the inability of women who have grown up with low self-esteem to find help in overcoming this debilitating problem. Traditionally, and due to society's view of the role of women, females resigned themselves for decades to being helpers, caretakers, homemakers, people who supported their husbands, making it easier for men to focus on their career goals. Parents followed this trend by discouraging their daughters from pursuing careers, from furthering their education, from studying such subjects as math and science and by trying to squelch the idea that women should expect to make money equal to that of men. And while we may think that things have changed, this was not so long ago and is far from completely altered. At their job, women are still frequently relegated to "support" or "helping" roles as secretaries or assistants, unable to rise to upper positions in their careers even though they are often more competent than their male bosses. A much smaller number of women have been able to climb the career ladder, even reaching positions where they are vice presidents of the divisions or departments of large companies; very few, however, ever reach the top unless it is in a business they themselves have built from the ground up.

Women today are fortunate to make 80 cents compared to every dollar men make, even when they have the same responsibilities at work and the same financial responsibilities at home. In addition to receiving lower compensation and fewer rewards, women continue to suffer harassment at their job and most often are not supported by those in charge when they complain; instead, a woman who makes an issue of harassment is often punished for speaking up. They are often omitted from important decision-making because such conclusions are reached on the golf course, in the spa, or in the locker room—places where women are not welcome or not invited. Women also talk about how their suggestions and comments are ignored, that men monopolize conversations in mixed groups. They feel belittled in these situations; they have difficulty maintaining their motivation and their morale.

The following are additional examples of how women are unfairly treated, even today: a) A stigma is attached to women who strive to rise to the top of businesses or who make a success of businesses they have started. b) Women are criticized who demand equal pay for equal work. Several colleges have been successfully sued in recent years by women coaches who only received equal pay to their male counterparts when they forced the colleges to do so. c) In college and high school sports, men are still hired to coach girl's and women's teams but can anyone imagine a woman being hired to coach men? d) Women have to work much harder than men to receive recognition and promotions. One of the most successful women entrepreneurs of our time has been harshly and unfairly criticized for behaviors that people take for granted, overlook, or even praise in men who have run their business in a similar fashion. So, don't be fooled into thinking that women in the U.S. enjoy equality. They simply do not.

Though many changes have taken place, certain religions, too, have had grave impact on the self-esteem of women. Many who subscribe to specific religious tenets still believe that men are superior to women, that they have rights women should not have, such as leading, speaking out, and being heard, implying that women cannot think as well as men, cannot reason as well as men, or have no place in leadership.. These religious organizations find support in their respective Bibles, manuals for why women should be in menial roles—and many women continue to bow to these man-made rules, so much so that they police other women who do not toe the line.

In the past, men prevented women from receiving an education, and for decades they did not "allow" women to vote. Whether or not you want to believe it, men actually used irrational arguments, suggesting that women's brains were smaller than those of men or that the tedium of studying would be too taxing to women's reproductive systems. When colleges first began admitting women, which largely occurred in the twentieth century, female students were not at first permitted to work toward degrees but were awarded lesser certificates. And they were only eventually allowed en masse into the work force during World War II, when the men were absent and bodies were needed to keep production lines moving.[2]

While some of this disturbing information may be new to you, this is not the author's personal view. And this is not male-bashing, folks; this is history and is well documented. History explains the way men have cruelly dominated women and discouraged their development. Today, while many young girls are growing up in homes that espouse equality, most women in the work force remain the casualties of such earlier ideologies.

Thus, women have had to fight for the gains they now have, all the while bearing the brunt of an unwelcoming society. Women have been stepped on, shoved aside, and repeatedly told they are overstepping their bounds. Some men will question or disagree with these facts, but let them ask themselves this: Would they ever vote for a female for President? This may, indeed, be the ultimate test of whether women have achieved equality in the thinking of the majority of our citizens. Until such time, many women, especially those with LSE, continue to feel like second-class citizens.

[2] Sadker, Myra and David Sadker. Failing at Fairness: How Our Schools Cheat Girls. Touchstone: New York, 1995, pp. 15-41.

Women continue to be told they are too pushy if they are assertive, too critical if they attempt to be managers, too "mouthy" if they offer their opinions, and too overbearing if they disagree. While many battles have been won and the victories are mounting in the fight for equality, many women have not had the strength or the support to even engage in it; many have succumbed to the pressure and expectations of this male-oriented society, damaged and deflated.

Now women who are enlightened about the way women have been treated, seek relationships in which they and their partners agree that both are equal; women with healthy self-esteem are highly motivated to accept nothing less.

- *A note of comparison with people who are healthy:*

Healthy people form relationships in which there exists mutual respect a willingness to negotiate fairly, sensitivity to the needs of both partners, a desire and willingness to regularly nurture and work on the relationship. They are people who are supportive, encouraging, cooperative, interesting, communicative, assertive, and open to change. Their relationships are fulfilling, though not all-encompassing in their lives. Healthy men seek female partners who are their equals. They are neither threatened by, nor fearful of the opinions, ideas, careers, or independence of strong women but see such a person as a welcome addition to their lives. Such secure men do not expect their wives/ partners to take a back seat to their careers; instead, the couple works together when career demands on each other change. They share in the responsibilities of creating a lifestyle they both enjoy; they both contribute energy to maintaining their home, family, friends, and activities. Their relationships are not dominated by traditional roles but rather function as a result of discussion and consensus based on their abilities, times, and other demands.

RECOVERY

People with LSE can learn to be content alone. It may be unimaginable at the moment, but many have developed this skill and have found their lives positively changed as a result. Unfortunately, like most things that are worthwhile, developing this ability to be alone takes time.

In addition, those who are now in unequal relationships can reconstruct those relationships if both people are quality, fair-minded individuals. If, however, one of the partners does not want an equal relationship, the relationship will never be entirely whole or healthy.

Those of us who suffer from LSE owe it to ourselves to insist upon nothing less than equality in a relationship. To accept anything else is to doom ourselves to a lifetime of low self-esteem in which we will sacrifice ourselves and our happiness while forfeiting the possibility of a truly intimate and fulfilling relationship.

THINGS TO DO

Exercise 1

All of us need to come to terms with our ability to be content alone. Seeking a relationship in order to alleviate our discontent with ourselves is another self-defeating endeavor. We must first learn to be alone—then and only then can we be a good partner to someone else—because then we can look for a relationship because we want one, not out of a need to feel complete.

If you have been thinking you want to be in a relationship or if you are starting one now, do this exercise to evaluate why. Understanding your motivation may make the difference in a wise or disastrous choice.

1. Determine why you want to be in this relationship: Ask your self:

   - Am I afraid to be alone? Am I looking for someone who can provide me with security?

   - Do I feel inadequate being alone? Am I looking for some one else to prove my self-worth?

   - Do I feel embarrassed being alone? Do I fear that others think negatively of me because I am alone?

   - Do I think being in a relationship will make me whole?

   - Do I think being in a relationship will solve the problems in my life?

   - Is being in a relationship the goal of my life?

Being in a relationship is not a solution to a personal problem—in fact, relationships pose a whole new set of problems as a couple works out the many details involved. If you discover that you have been thinking of a relationship as the answer for your life, look elsewhere to satisfy your unhappiness—look at yourself and begin to deal with your issues.

2. Analyze the particular relationship you are forming (or if you are not in a relationship yet, consider what important ingredients will be necessary for you to be in one.) As the relationship continues, ask yourself the following questions:

   • Does this relationship enhance my life?

   • Does it allow for my individuality to develop or grow?

   • Is it based on mutual respect?

   • Is it honest, with open and direct communication?

   • Does it provide me with a sense of being loved, nurtured, respected?

   • Does it provide for the best interests of each of us?

   • Does the other person have any specific problems that could interfere with a good relationship, e.g., alcohol, unfinished prior relationship, financial problems, etc.?

3. Look for inconsistencies or lack of truthfulness in the relationship. If these exist, step back and reevaluate. Don't take these lightly—they're usually more important than they look. Trust your gut. Don't make allowances or overlook the signs. Many people later say they saw such indications but didn't take them seriously.

4. Look at your own behavior and emotions since the beginning of the relationship and ask yourself:

    - Have I changed since beginning this relationship? Is that change for the better?

    - Am I giving up things that I used to enjoy for this relationship? Do I think this is in my best interest?

    - Am I happier and more content now? Or more troubled and anxious?

    - Do my emotions fluctuate more now?

    - Have I maintained some separateness in my life (e.g., friends, interests, goals) since beginning this relationship?

5. Above all, be honest with yourself about the relationship.

If you recognize that you are seeking out a relationship for the wrong reasons, you've just been given a red light, which means stop what you are doing. These red lights indicate you need to look more closely to discern the seriousness of the problem; red lights mean stop and may also indicate that you change direction immediately. Experiencing frequent red lights is an indication that you need to have a better understanding of yourself and your motives—that you need to focus on your own personal development before continuing your efforts to enter into a relationship.

THINGS TO DO

Exercise 2

People with LSE tend to discount their own strengths and achievements. While few people will ever be the best at anything, all of us have indeed developed skills—we are likely more capable than we were five years ago. To begin the process of developing self-respect, it is important to become aware of the skills and abilities we now possess. It is helpful to be cognizant of our past achievements. This exercise will assist you in recognizing these positive accomplishments.

1. Make a list of your skills, your past achievements, and things you've learned about your abilities. For example, do you cook, speak foreign languages, play tennis, or do woodworking? Are you creative? Do you draw, paint, write poetry? Have you decorated your home or landscaped your yard? (If you have difficulty with this task, ask someone who's known you a long time, someone who knows you well, a friend, a loved one, or your therapist to help you compile your list.)

2. Write your list on a 3 x 5 card. Carry the card with you at all times.

3. Five times a day read the list to yourself, preferably aloud.

4. Do this for 60 days. *Important:* Do not skip a day.

5. Continue adding to your list as you become aware of more strengths, skills, or past achievements.

6. At the end of each week,take your list and while looking in the mirror, use each word or phrase to complete this sentence: "I have learned to cook" or "I have become a gardener" or "I am learning to fish" or "I have received a promotion" or "I speak

French" or "I play golf" or "I am taking classes to improve my skills for work" or "I earned a college degree in math" or "I have received a good raise at work" or "I have become more involved in my community" or "I have made a new friend" or "I read 3 new books recently" or "I walked in the Race for the Cure"— whatever the words, make them into a sentence.

Say it with conviction. Go through your entire list this way. Do this weekly for 60 days.

How did you feel doing this exercise? Was it difficult to make your list? Did you feel uncomfortable saying these positive things about yourself? Did you believe them when you said them? Did you try to minimize them or discount them in some way? Did it become easier after a few days? Were you able to add to your list?

In time you will find this exercise easier. You will begin to believe what you are saying. You will appreciate the skills that you possess and the things you have accomplished. Remember, every new skill and achievement is growth!

THINGS TO DO

Exercise 3

If you would like to establish a "two become three" relationship with your present partner, in either a committed or developing relationship, try the following:

1. Sit down and discuss the model together until you feel you both understand how it works.

2. Make a commitment that you will each abide by the specific distinctions of the model.

3. Discuss where your present relationship differs from the model and how your relationship will look if it works as the model suggests.

4. Discuss the areas in your relationship that might need to be changed.

5. Together, develop a plan of how you will change one specific area.

   - What specific behaviors will be involved?

   - What will be required of each person?

   - How will you make each other aware if you revert to your present patterns?

6. Select another area that needs to be changed and follow Step 5.

7. Set up a regular time to sit down and reevaluate your progress.

If you are in a developing relationship with a person who is not willing to comply with this model, take a close look at this information. There is one primary reason why a person would not want this type relationship—he or she does not want equality. This is a sure sign of an unhealthy attitude, one that will not lead to a healthy relationship, one that can only lead to the other person's unhappiness. Do not continue this relationship; do not make allowances for the other adult; do not think you can change that person. Get out of this relationship and determine to choose only a future partner who willingly and freely prescribes to this model.

6

Listening to and Controlling Our Inner Voice

JANE: negative self-statements

Following her divorce, Jane became aware that she had given up all of her friends; she had no one to talk to, no support group, and she was very lonely. She decided that she wanted to meet some women that she could relate to, but she was unsure of how to do this. Finally, after considering different options, she joined a book group that read and discussed selected new publications. In this group she met Harriet, a woman she soon learned who was also divorced and without children. She admired Harriet and felt she would be able to relate to her but became riddled with apprehension about initiating a relationship. One day she would be determined to ask Harriet to coffee following the next meeting, but when the time came, Jane would say to herself, "Why would Harriet want to be friends with me? I bet she sees me as boring. What would I even have to talk about?" As her anxiety grew, her inner voice escalated with statements like "She probably has lots of friends, she won't want to spend time with me. What made me think she would like me anyway? She seems so 'together,' and when she realizes that I'm not, she won't want to spend time with me."

Weeks went by with Jane trying to get up the courage to approach Harriet, until finally one evening when Jane and Harriet were walking out of the building together, Harriet turned to Jane and said, "I've been meaning to ask you if you would like to get together sometime. I've enjoyed meeting you and have appreciated your comments in study group. I think we may have a lot in common." Surprise registered on Jane's face while inside she felt excited. She turned to Harriet and said enthusiastically, "I'd love to get together with you. Actually, I've had the same idea, but I guess I was just too shy to bring it up. I thought you were probably already too busy." The women then made plans to meet the following Saturday for lunch.

Jane nearly missed this opportunity to get to know Harriet, because in her head she had talked herself out of the idea. By telling herself negative things, she raised the anxiety and fear that she would be rejected. If Harriet had not initiated getting together, this opportunity might well have been lost.

Self-Talk

What we say to ourselves dictates how we feel, what we believe, and ultimately what we do. Whether or not we are aware of it, we talk to ourselves constantly. Silently and only to ourselves, we make comments about the things we observe about others and the things we see in ourselves, including our expectations of self and others. Most people are not very aware of this ongoing internal conversation, nor are they aware of the profound effect of this personal monologue.

It is actually here in our minds that we form our interpretations (usually distorted for those with LSE) and give ourselves feedback (usually negative) through our inner voice. Here in our heads, we review and critically evaluate ourselves—our words, our actions, our appearance, our competence. And it is in this process that we either produce turmoil and anxiety (the usual pattern for LSE sufferers) or quiet our fears and encourage confidence (the normal pattern for those with healthy self-esteem). As a result, these thinking processes become the motivation for how we proceed in life.

If you gain only one thing from this book, I want it to be an increased awareness and understanding of the fact that:

- You talk to yourself constantly.

- You become the architect and creator of the emotions you later experience through this self-talk.

- Your self-talk, if not monitored for accuracy, becomes the impetus for continual self-sabotage.

Emotions do not come as the result of an observation or an experience but rather as the result of the things we conclude and then say to ourselves about those perceptions or situations. Thus, two people can have the same experience or observe the same event and come away with very different opinions and emotions. The results are dependent upon our cognitive interpretations and are often based on our past experiences.

Example:

> *Sue grew up in an upper middle-class home where alcohol was offered to most visitors and drinks were served before and after meals, though no one was considered alcoholic or even a heavy drinker. She assumed everyone did this. When she graduated from college and got her own apartment, one of the*

things she did in getting settled was to stock her bar. She purchased a variety of glasses to accommodate different drinks and a wide assortment of liquors. Though she had seldom had a drink since leaving home, she purchased these alcoholic beverages nonchalantly, thinking of it as a necessity for entertaining rather than a preference for alcohol.

A few months later, Sue began dating Tim, a premed student at the university 60 miles away. Sue had met Tim's parents on three occasions when they had come to see him, and she decided it was time to invite them and Tim to her place for dinner. Tim was particularly pleased by Jane's thoughtfulness. He agreed to come for the weekend, his parents for dinner on Sunday.

When everyone arrived, Sue offered drinks, announcing the available possibilities. Tim's father hesitated and then said he would have a beer. Tim also agreed to a beer; his mother declined anything. Sue fixed herself a gin and tonic.

At dinner Sue served wine, which everyone sipped politely. After Tim and his parents refused a refill, Sue poured herself what was left in order to finish the bottle. She thought she saw Tim's mother give his father a strange frown, which made her uncomfortable. Yet everyone raved about her dinner and she felt more relaxed, deciding that she must have imagined that something was wrong.

Tim had said his parents loved to play table games, so Sue suggested they all play scrabble. As the perfect hostess, Sue again offered a round of drinks. Her guests exchanged glances and declined. Sue was relieved since she didn't really want another drink herself but would have joined them to be polite. She returned to the game; but the remainder of the evening she felt tension in the air but had no idea what it meant.

The following week Tim called to say he was going to be exceptionally busy for a few weeks and really wouldn't have time to spend with her. Sue thought he sounded different on the phone but decided he was just stressed with all he had to do. The remainder of the week, however, Tim did not call. This was unusual, so Sue tried him at the dorm but couldn't reach him. He didn't return her call and didn't call the following week. Now Sue was worried—what had happened? What did this mean?

Sue is unaware that her family's customs and expectations around alcohol are not shared by all families. She views her family's habits as merely social drinking and not a problem. She has not been around people whose lives have been negatively affected or destroyed by alcohol. She knows she has blundered in some way but doesn't know how, and because Tim won't return her phone calls, she may never find out.

In fact, Tim comes from a family that has seen its share of alcohol-related problems. His brother has been in treatment and is divorced as a result, and Tim has an uncle whose death was alcohol- related. His family is one in which the only alcohol in the home consisted of an occasional six-pack of beer or wine served on a holiday. When his family saw Sue's supply of liquor and her knowledge of mixed drinks, etc., they were immediately apprehensive and suspicious. They strongly advised Tim to sever the relationship, suggesting that if she openly drank this much in front of his family, she must be drinking consistently in her life.

Tim's family have a different perspective than Sue. They draw conclusions, based on the environment from which they have come, in this case one that has experienced tragedy because of alcohol. They observe her behavior and interpret it as a serious problem.

Distorted Thinking

Not all people are aware that others may perceive things differently, but the truth is that both those with healthy and low self-esteem view circumstances in a variety of ways. Many misunderstandings arise because people assume that others think like they do and see situations in the same light; consequently, they do not ask for clarification or discuss the discrepancy in their views. People with LSE make these same assumptions; they do not recognize that their perceptions and interpretations are largely due to the specific environment they grew up in and that others may not share their perspective.

When we talk to ourselves, we experience feelings that coincide with our self-talk; we are certain that our analysis is correct and we believe what we are saying. Thus, what we say, we believe, and then we experience the emotions that coincide with that belief. For instance, if we say to ourselves statements that indicate we are not very "smart," we will believe these statements and we will likely feel inadequate. Then the next time we are asked for an opinion on a subject that we think requires intelligence to answer, we may be frightened to share our opinion, thinking we don't have the capability to make an informed response.

Making the situation even more complicated for those of us with LSE is the fact that our self-talk is affected by our distorted filtering system. As a result, the statement we make to ourselves will not only be one of many possible normal interpretations but may produce conclusions that are inaccurate or at least partially distorted.

Example:

Kathy cooks a meal for her partner, Jackie, on Thursday evening, while her friend Evelyn cooks for her family. Each tries out the same new recipe. Each has the same results—it's not very good— but quite different reactions. Kathy tells herself that the meal was barely edible, labels herself a "terrible cook," and berates herself, saying she must have done something wrong again. Evelyn tells herself that she didn't like that recipe, must mark it in the book so she doesn't fix it again, and is glad she didn't try it out on company. Kathy is disgusted with herself while Evelyn's feelings about herself are neutral.

Each had the same experience (the failed recipe), but Kathy takes personal responsibility for it and chastises herself. Evelyn blames the recipe and feels fine about herself. Kathy's doubts about her competence lead her to jump to the conclusion that she must have done something wrong; she makes negative statements to herself about her lack of skills, believes these remarks, and then experiences feelings that match. (Placing the blame on herself is an automatic reaction for a person with LSE.) Consequently, Kathy comes away from the cooking experiment feeling discouraged and negative about herself.

Example:

Sara is slender, shapely, and attractive, though she is unaware that others actually perceive her this way for she has quite a different view of herself. In her mind, Sara sees bulging thighs and an unattractive nose. When she goes shopping for a pair of slacks, she stands in front of the mirror turning this way and that way, glaring at her thighs; she feels miserable and ugly. The clerk at first comments on how well the slacks fit and how nice Sara looks in them, but Sara gives her a disgusted glance, once again looking at her thighs, which she tells herself are huge.

A friend who has accompanied Sara on this shopping trip shakes her head in dismay as she listens to Sara berate herself. The clerk rolls her eyes and says, "We should all have such problems." Sara doesn't believe what she is hearing; she has told herself for so long that she is fat that she believes it to be true. Even her eyes register this distortion of the facts. She thinks the clerk is just trying to make a sale. "She must be on commission," Sara tells herself.

While all of us have this inner voice, those with LSE frequently arrive at conclusions that are not based on the facts. Sara dismisses the remarks of the clerk, who tells her she looks great in the slacks, and judges herself through her own negative perceptions, a judgment that is not valid. Telling herself something that is not true (she has big thighs) creates feelings that coincide with these self-statements (she is miserable; she is disgusted with the clerk's comments), though these emotions do not parallel the truth. Her actions are then a result of how she thinks and feels—she is obsessed with her appearance and seems to others to be overly self-focused. This pervasive form of irrationality is a central issue for those who suffer from LSE. This inner voice causes our video to become distorted and can continue—throughout our lives—to twist the facts so that they conform to our damaged self-image. In the beginning, it is very difficult for those of us with LSE to overcome the habits we have of constantly making negative self-statements.

To correct this obsessive behavior, we must learn to do the following:

• Realize that our method is faulty. (It is very difficult to accept that the way we have spoken to ourselves all these years is a dysfunctional means of self-evaluation. We must force ourselves to believe the facts rather than allow ourselves to rely on our emotional reactions to distorted thoughts. Sara is not fat by any factual data.)

• Evaluate our self-statements only on the basis of whether they are factual (can we prove it?), truthful (do we know it to be the truth from experience?), or historical (does it fit a pattern that's been established?), rather than on the basis of past feed back or abuse from dysfunctional people in our youth.

• Realize that when we have LSE, our thinking is often distorted, making our process invalid and our deductions inaccurate.

- Eventually and over time, become aware of the distortion *at the actual time we are saying it.* (As Sara looks in the mirror, she must ask herself, "What are the facts about my thighs?")

- Determine to alter our dysfunctional pattern of negatively inaccurate self-talk.

- Begin questioning each negative self-statement for its validity based on fact, truth, or history.

- Determine what to say instead that is accurate. (Sara could replace her negative statement with an accurate one such as "I have a good figure.")

- Practice replacing distorted statements that we regularly say with more accurate ones. (Before going shopping and while standing in front of the mirror at home, Sara could say, "I know I tend to see myself as fat but that's really not true. When I go shopping today, I will not make negative statements to myself about my figure, or if I do, I will try to replace them immediately.")

This process means changing the way we have communicated with ourselves our entire lives and ultimately means editing our videotape and producing one that is more accurate. This may sound simple; it is not. It entails a battle with ourselves at every juncture. It means changing a process that we may not even be aware we are engaged in. It requires developing a more objective perspective; learning to be an optimist, when maybe we've always been the opposite. (Note: While this book is mainly intended to be an overview of what LSE is and how it is formed, it also provides insight, exercises, and suggestions into how to begin the recovery process. More of this process is discussed in my workbook, *The Personal Workbook for Breaking the Chain of Low Self-Esteem* and in *The Self-Esteem Recovery Toolkit.*)

Difficulty Sleeping

People with LSE often talk of how they obsessively review the day's events each night. Many will say they cannot get to sleep because they lie awake evaluating their day: what occurred, what they and others said or didn't say, what others meant by what they said or didn't say. It seems the stillness of night, when they cannot avoid looking at themselves, allows their anxiety to surface and take control. As they review their behavior, they criticize the areas where they believe they should have done something differently; because their view of themselves is negative, this review almost always has a disapproving tone. At the end of the day, this critical analysis interferes with rest; they then awaken emotionally exhausted and discouraged. Beginning the new day in this condition, fatigued and dwelling on memories that are not affirming, results in more negative thinking throughout the day.

Two Extremes: Superiority and Inferiority

Like a pendulum on a clock, people with low self-esteem swing back and forth between extremes in the attitudes they have and responses they make to various situations. One such extreme is feeling superior to others vs. feeling inferior to others. They may actually see themselves as inferior at one point and as superior later, or they may feel inferior in one setting and superior in another. They try to gauge how well they are doing in life by comparing themselves to others, which is, unfortunately, not a wise strategy. We can always find someone who is superior or inferior to ourselves in some respect; to use this information as a basis for self-evaluation is both destructive and inaccurate.

Because those with LSE can respond at either extreme of feeling superior or inferior, the fact that their behavior is related to low self-esteem is not always recognizable to the casual observer. While one can understand why a person with low self-esteem views himself as inferior to others, it may seem incongruous that such a person would feel superior to others. In fact, though, they do exist and are often seen as haughty or as "know-it-alls." They may also appear to be argumentative, opinionated, obnoxious, proud, arrogant, and dogmatic—not qualities most people would associate with low self-esteem.

In addition, those with low self-esteem are often exceptionally critical and focus on the weaknesses and mistakes of others to make themselves feel better. Throughout life, we see people make the common mistake of thinking they can elevate themselves by verbally castigating someone else, either in action or word. In the moment, this may make the accuser feel better about himself, but the unseen damage is one of erosion of the person's own self-respect—for when we put others down, we really put ourselves down even more by opting to use these tactics. The people who do this are reacting to their LSE from a position of superiority; rather than recognizing that they just have certain skills that others do not, they may openly and proudly state they see themselves as better than others.

Example:

Jack has low self-esteem. His fellow workers do not like him and have complained to his supervisor on several occasions. They feel he is sullen, rude, overbearing, and unavailable for their questions. Jack tells himself that these problems are caused by his coworkers, who want to chat all the time instead of focusing on their work like he does. He thinks it is all right to respond to them the way he does, saying to himself, "A stupid question deserves a stupid answer or no answer at all. They are all idiots."

Jack's boss, however, has also confronted him on several occasions about the quality of his work. Jack dismisses these encounters by telling himself that the boss is totally incompetent and shouldn't even be a supervisor.

This attitude of superiority is a typical reaction, a defense mechanism whereby Jack defends himself against other deeper feelings of inadequacy. He knows his coworkers do not like him but he is unwilling to look at his own behavior; instead, he rationalizes there is something wrong with them.

Example:

Ryan is an executive who feels inferior in social settings but feels superior to others in his work. Consequently, he spends 60 hours or more at his job, where he feels most comfortable. He frequently uses work-related excuses to avoid attending social engagements with his wife and family. Because he avoids this area of his life, he does not grow socially. Social engagements that cannot be ignored continue to cause him excruciating fear and anxiety, to which he responds by working even more.

Ryan is able to ignore his areas of weakness by devoting his time and energy to the more comfortable places in his life. For Ryan, avoiding what is difficult is self-destructive and allows him to maintain a false sense of who he is, while denying him the opportunity to grow by embracing social opportunities. As he concentrates on and further develops his strengths, his weaknesses remain intact.

Figure 4: Two extremes: Superiority and Inferiority

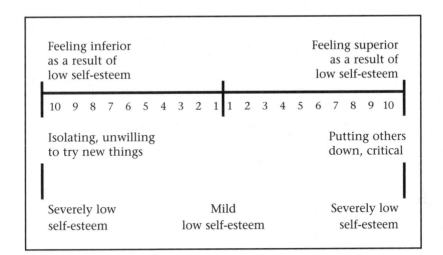

Figure 3 above shows how those with low self-esteem fall at either end of the spectrum. The high numbers indicate individuals with more severe conditions of low self-esteem, while the lower numbers indicate the less severe experience. The higher the number, the more inferior or superior a person may feel and act in response to his environment.

Below are examples of how people respond to their LSE in either a superior or inferior way. Both lists represent equally dysfunctional behaviors and attitudes of the extreme reactions of those with LSE.

Ways a person takes on a superior stance:

• Believing you know what's best for another person, i.e., "What you should do is. . ."

• Trying to control the lives of others

- Putting down the ideas or opinions of others

- Bragging about your own skills and achievements

- Believing that you can do anything better than others

- Focusing on skills you have that others don't have

- Being rigid in thinking you know the answers

- Being closed to suggestions from others

- Treating others as though they are beneath you

- Ignoring or ridiculing a person's feelings

- Barely listening to what someone is saying because you are so focused on what you want to say when they finish

- Giving unsolicited advice to other adults

Ways a person responds from an inferior position:

- Avoiding people, activities, new experiences (out of fear of rejection, criticism, or failure)

- Relying on others for the answers (fear of making wrong decisions)

- Giving up goals, dreams, or control of your life

- Focusing on skills others have that you don't

- Deferring to others

- Refraining from sharing opinions, ideas, and perceptions

- Lying

- Allowing others to take advantage of you

- Tolerating abuse

- Being unwilling to ask for help from others when there's something you don't know how to do

- Being unwilling to go to therapy when areas of your life are not working well

- Thinking and acting as though your wants and feelings don't matter

Comparison with Others

Comparing themselves to others is a practice people with LSE often use to rate their own sufficiency, albeit a dysfunctional and destructive one. Unfortunately, when people use comparison as a means of self-evaluation, those in the inferior mode generally only compare themselves with people who have more: have accomplished more, are better known or liked, have made more money, or done more, those who are further along in their development or careers. When those with LSE determine that they are far less adequate than these people, they then berate themselves; they produce more negative self-statements.

In contrast, those in the superior mode who have LSE only compare themselves with those who have less, who don't perform as well, or who are less skilled. In this way, they can maintain their distorted fantasy that they are superior to others. Seldom do people with low self-esteem compare themselves to those like themselves, who come from similar backgrounds, who have had comparable opportunities for development. Furthermore, because comparison, like competition, implies that one wins and one loses, using comparison in this fashion means losing for those who already picture themselves as inadequate and means winning for those who see themselves as winners (those who feel superior). Knowing that others make more money, have more friends, receive promotions and recognition more often, are more capable, have greater intelligence, or are better liked does not enhance a person's feelings about himself, if it is the means by which he measures his own worth. Depending on the category of comparison, he will feel less adequate in that part of his life. (Or, when in the superior mode, he will feel more adequate.) Neither is a healthy means of self-evaluation.

Comparing ourselves to another person is like comparing apples to oranges. A healthier way to gauge our development is to compare our output or accomplishments with our own status in the past. In other words, it is prudent to ask ourselves if we have improved, grown, changed, developed, or increased our production in comparison to a selected date in our past. This means of evaluation takes into consideration where we began, our growth up to a certain point, and our achievement to date; it is not based on contrast with others.

Feelings Can be Changed

It is, of course, ridiculous to tell people not to feel the way they do, for we are not able to change our feelings simply by telling ourselves to feel differently. Consequently, we become even more discouraged when someone says, "You shouldn't feel that way" or "Don't feel bad about that"; we perceive that we are being criticized for what, to us, is an authentic and valid experience over which we have no control; we feel others are telling us there is something wrong with us for feeling the way we do or that our feelings are not important. Since our emotional experience is the result of our cognitive processes, we can, however, learn to restructure our thinking by replacing negative, irrational thoughts with positive, rational ones; then our feelings will be different. By altering our thinking, we will eventually find that our feelings follow suit. (For the purpose of discussion about low self-esteem, rational thoughts or statements are confined to those that are based on fact, truth, or history. Irrational thoughts or self-statements are not.)

Example:

Overweight and apprehensive about attending his 30-year high school reunion, Sig remembers how his classmates used to joke about people who were heavy. Unsure if they will actually voice their observations about him, he nevertheless fears their reactions. "Even if they don't let it show, they will be laughing at me," he tells himself. "They may even make comments when they see me like, 'Put on a little weight, haven't you, Sig?'" He begins to berate himself for allowing the pounds to accrue. "What is the matter with me that I can't control my eating? Why don't I exercise regularly like other people do? What is wrong with me?" Already struggling with feelings of inadequacy and insecurity, Sig wrestles with whether or not to attend the reunion. He feels discouraged and disgusted with himself.

Then Sig catches himself, realizing he has been focusing on negative, self-defeating statements. In therapy, Sig has been learning how destructive this kind of self-talk is, and he makes a conscious decision to change what he is saying to himself. He decides that he must stick to the facts. Concentrating on these facts, he says, "It's true that I have put on a few pounds since high school, but most people do as they get older. While I am heavier, I don't look bad and I feel great. My partner, Annie, says she likes the way I look, that I was too thin before. At least I'm not going bald yet; I still have all my hair. I've done okay since high school; I've got a wonderful family and a good job and I'm even on the local school board. I really have nothing to be ashamed of. What does it matter what these people think? If they are so shallow that all they see is my weight, why should I care? It would be fun to see the old gang. In fact, I'd like them to meet my family. I certainly don't care how they look and I'd like to hear what they've been doing. I think I do want to go to the reunion. It will be fun."

Sig picks up the phone to call Annie at her job. "Annie, I've decided I do want to go to the class reunion. I want to show off you and the kids." "Great," Annie responds, "call and get the plane reservations."

Sig had the power to produce feelings about his reunion that would either encourage him to go or discourage him so much that he would remain home. In the past, these self-statements regularly impacted his behavior negatively, so much so that his wife had recommended therapy. After dragging his heels, Sig decided she was right and began his search for the right therapist, someone who specializes in recovery from LSE. Nine months down the road, he is making significant changes in his life, fully supported by Annie and by his therapist.

During these months of therapy, Sig has developed skills that often enable him to identify the negative spiral he experiences, a spiral largely due to his own self-talk. He is even frequently able to turn that negative thinking into positive thinking as he did here. Sig is much happier and finds that his moods do not fluctuate to the extremes they did in the past.

- *A note of comparison with those with healthy self-esteem:*

People with healthy self-esteem do not obsessively review their behavior, nor are they highly critical of their daily performance when they do look back on it. They assume they will act in ways that are consistent with their standards and values appropriately and are generally pleased with their behavior. Even when they occasionally wish they had done or said something differently, they do not beat up on themselves; instead, they devise a plan to correct the problem or think of how they will respond differently the next time they are in a similar situation. They do not continue to dwell on the problem endlessly.

People with healthy self-esteem praise themselves and often review their successes in their minds. They may say to themselves, "Good job, Jean, I think you'll get that promotion," or "You fixed a tasty meal tonight and I think everyone really enjoyed it." They do not wrestle with excessive anxiety about the past nor the future. They use past mistakes as springboards to improve and grow. They are usually pleased with themselves and are aware that others like and respect them.

RECOVERY

For those who suffer from LSE, the goal must be recovery! One cannot merely "raise" self-esteem, for that only means finding a way to feel better about yourself for a time. Recovery means erasing the dysfunctional videotape and replacing it with a description of ourselves that is factual, truthful, and based on our record. Recovery means removing the self-doubt, eliminating the self-recrimination, and ultimately changing the basics of how we see ourselves so that the view we have of self is accurate and reliable. Recovery means starting over in our awareness of what goals we could reach, what dreams we could realize, and what life would be like without constant fear and anxiety. The following describes the steps to recovery:

1. We must become aware that we talk to ourselves constantly.

2. We must be willing to admit that our self-talk, if negative or anxiety-provoking, is likely distorted.

3. We must realize that our emotions are the result of our self-talk.

4. We must recognize that we have control over our self-talk and thus indirect control over our emotions.

5. We must focus intently and regularly on recognizing specifically what we say to ourselves.

6. We must consistently and relentlessly focus on questioning the veracity of our self-statements; i.e., are they based on fact, truth, or history?

7. We must then strive to alter these inaccurate statements so that we are only telling ourselves things that are accurate.

8. We must seek help if we cannot do these difficult steps on our own.

THINGS TO DO

Exercise 1

If you have difficulty sleeping because negative self-statements bombard you, try the following:

1. List your most favorite memories, e.g., your favorite vacation, most outstanding achievement, most enjoyable afternoon or weekend, or happiest moment.

2. If you are presently too discouraged to think of a pleasant memory, list places you would like to visit some day or things you would like to do.

3. Keep these lists by your bed.

4. Before you turn out the light, choose two from your lists. As soon as the light is out and your head hits the pillow, focus on one of your chosen items. If it is a past favorite vacation, for example, slowly think through that vacation: How did you decide to go? How did you get there? Who was with you? What did you do? Focus on all the specific details of the trip, especially the positive memories.

5. Do not allow any thoughts to change your focus. If irrelevant thoughts interfere, acknowledge them and then go back to the details of your vacation.

6. If you have thought of everything you possibly can about that wonderful vacation and you are still awake, move on to your second selection.

7. Try to keep all your thoughts positive.

8. Do this exercise as often as necessary.

At first, it may be difficult for you to concentrate on this exercise. Unwanted thoughts may keep reappearing. In time, however, you will be able to control your thoughts and this exercise will help you to get the rest you need.

THINGS TO DO

Exercise 2

To begin the process of altering your self-talk, try the following:

1. When you realize you are upset, try to remember the exact statements you have been making to yourself. Be specific. Write these statements down. This may be difficult to do at first, but keep trying. We make these comments to ourselves so automatically that you may have difficulty remembering them at first or recognizing them for what they are.

2. Look at your list of self-statements. Since you were distraught when you began to analyze them, they will be negative. If the statements you have written down are not negative, you haven't found them yet. Keep thinking. Remember "awareness" is the first and most crucial step in acquiring any new skill—it also may take time to develop.

3. When you have been able to delineate one or more negative self-statements, ask yourself if each is accurate. Most likely, all or at least part of the statement is not. If you cannot recognize the inaccurate parts, ask a friend to help you or talk to your therapist about your statements.

4. Once you have determined which parts of your statements are not true, replace them with ones that are. Repeat these newly phrased sentences to yourself. If you do this exercise correctly, you will eventually begin to feel better about the specific situation you are evaluating and better about yourself.

5. Make a commitment to yourself that you are going to stop irrational self-talk (any statements that are not factual, truthful, or based on history).

Note: This is not an easy exercise nor is it a simple process; in fact, most people may need the help of a therapist skilled in self-esteem recovery, at least to get started. Since you have been thinking the way you do for most of your life, recovery will not be quick or easy but will require persistence, determination, and a willingness to stick to it. Be assured, however, those who have steadfastly dedicated their energies to such a recovery program have successfully reinvented themselves, becoming the people they were meant to be and realizing their true selves while discarding the lingering self-defeating tapes that had controlled their lives for so long. You too can overcome your negative and inaccurate self-perspective if you are determined to do so.

7

The Search for Unconditional Love

JANE: her mother

When Jane was a teenager, she was not only tall but quite heavy; being bigger than all of her friends made her very self-conscious. Both her parents were heavy as well and did nothing to help her learn proper eating habits or help her with her weight problem. In fact, her mother often made negative remarks about her weight, especially at meal times when she cooked big meals and then criticized Jane for eating too much. At the end of the meal when Jane, whose feelings were hurt, would refuse her mother's homemade pie, her mother would say, "Well, one piece of pie won't hurt you." Jane never understood these double messages.

Jane was a good student, well-liked, and energetic. She won awards and two scholarships, excelled in music, was All-Conference in volleyball, was one of the top in her class scholastically, and held down a part-time job throughout high school. She diligently did her chores at home, obeyed her parents' rules, and tried to make them proud.

*Jane's mother, however, was frequently critical of Jane in
other ways, finding fault with her hair and her friends, and how
she managed her money, even though Jane was very frugal. Over
the years, Jane tried hard to win her mother's approval—which
never came. She wondered why her mother treated her the way
she did, why she was so negative and judgmental. She decided
that her mother must not love her. She wondered what was so
wrong with her that her mother found her "unlovable."*

Feeling Unlovable

Those who have low self-esteem have one thing in common—
on some level, they share a deep-seated fear that there is something basically wrong with them and wonder if they may be
unlovable or unacceptable. This pervasive feeling is basic to the
development of low self-esteem, though people may not be conscious of it, unwilling to directly face the question. At the same
time, however, they may berate themselves in front of friends,
family, and coworkers or display self-sabotaging behaviors
(described in Chapter 4). Others become defensive, reacting to
their fears by appearing overly confident, even egotistical. All are
grappling with similar emotions and anxiety.

The idea that one may be at the core, unlovable, is devastating
to consider. Wondering if this is the reason for rejections by parents or peers, those with LSE easily become depressed, even hopeless and suicidal for periods. Others attempt to block out these
haunting questions; burying their feelings, they just go on. Some
strive for excellence, hoping achievement and success can silence
their condemning inner voice.

Self-esteem is first developed when as children we are taught
the difference between right and wrong, good and bad—when we
begin to develop individual skills and a picture of who we are.
When a child receives consistent feedback that he usually does
things "wrong," he begins to question his own competence. If he is

neglected, he feels unimportant; if he is laughed at, he feels foolish. He may feel like a failure, become discouraged and lethargic, losing his willingness to initiate and try. He may become dependent and compliant, believing others have the answers while he does not.

When we don't regularly receive praise and support for what we attempt or for who we are as individuals, we begin to question our basic adequacy. We become fearful, our ambition may be squelched, our creativity may be suppressed. We may feel afraid to try new things; we may learn not to take risks where we may be vulnerable to further criticism. When the child does not receive love and approval, she begins to question her ability to be loved, her lovability. She may lower her expectations for relationships or future happiness. She may feel hopeless and dejected, listlessly plodding through life.

This is the point at which personalities begin to react differently. Some begin to retreat; others become enraged and act out, determined to fight back in a attempt to cast off this undesirable label. Some become overachievers while others become underachievers. Some accept the identification tag thrust upon them and see themselves as inadequate, incompetent, unlovable. Most continue on their respective paths throughout their lives—combative or compliant.

The Need to Be Loved and Accepted

When we truly love someone in a healthy way, we allow that person to be an individual, with her own differing opinions. We encourage her to make her own decisions, to determine her own goals, to develop her own interests. We exhibit an interest in her chosen direction, listening to her opinions and ideas, expressing admiration of her progress. We respect her right to make these choices rather than believing we know what's best for her. We support her. We don't give unsolicited advice. We don't tease or ridicule her. We don't try to make her into a clone of ourselves.

Each of us has within us the need to be loved in this way, the need to know we are special to some and acceptable to most. When doubt replaces the fulfillment of that need, we are unable to be all that we have the potential to be, for we question what about us is lacking or missing—what about us is less than what others are. Unfortunately, that self-doubt, once ingrained, becomes the basis for our motivation or lack thereof, often throughout the remainder of our lives: This is the foundation for our low self-esteem. The question "Am I unlovable?" lingers—no matter how far it may be pushed into the recesses of our minds— for a day, a month, or a year. Sadly, it is the reason that once damaged, our low self-esteem can never be fully restored, though we can recover to the point of only rarely having self-esteem attacks and with the length and severity of those attacks being so reduced in magnitude that they have little impact on our lives. Thus, while we cannot predict when something will trigger a painful memory and while we therefore cannot completely wipe out the effects of a dysfunctional past, through recovery we can lead fully functioning lives, with a new understanding that we are lovable, competent, deserving, significant, and adequate.

Example:

When Kerry was five years old, her younger brother became very ill. For nearly four years, her parents' time was consumed with running to doctors and hospitals. Kerry was not allowed to go see her brother; instead, she was left with relatives and friends.

For periods of time her brother would be home, but even then his illness required constant monitoring and care—leaving little time to attend to Kerry's needs. At first Kerry felt very bad about her brother's problems. Over time, however, she began to resent him. She knew and understood very little about his condition, but she knew that it was because of him that her parents were never around.

When on occasion her parents were home, they were usually too tired or preoccupied to give her much attention. For Kerry, this was very confusing—she saw how much time they devoted to her brother and wanted their time and affection too. She would look forward to being with them but was disappointed because they hardly seemed to notice her. Promises they made to her were often broken; she began to wonder if they really loved her. Feeling abandoned and very lonely, Kerry grew up wishing her parents cared as much about her as they did about her brother.

Kerry developed low self-esteem from a form of neglect, even though it was not due to irresponsible behavior on the part of her parents. Along with maintaining their jobs, her parents were too consumed with their son's life-threatening illness to have sufficient time or energy for Kerry. They did not purposely ignore her but were too exhausted to give her the nurturing she needed. Hoping that their son's condition would soon improve and things would return to normal, they didn't realize that months and years of Kerry's life were passing by unnoticed—a period of time when her basic developmental needs were not being met.

By the time Kerry's brother recovered from his illness, Kerry was nearing her tenth birthday. During his illness, she had spent more time staying with other relatives and friends than in her own home. Shifting from place to place, she had no sense of belonging; she did not have a room that had been fixed up to represent her current age. With her clothes and personal things often left in different homes and later lost, Kerry had developed a sense that neither she nor her belongings were of much significance.

When children are not given love and acceptance, they blame this lack of nurturing on themselves, believing they must be unlovable. Why else would a mother not love her child? Why else would a father not nurture his son or daughter? Rather than focusing the blame on the cause—the parent's shortcomings, these children who don't feel powerful or who aren't mature enough to question their parent's behavior instead believe that the neglect, criticism, and abuse are all that they deserve—all that they are worthy of. Children, even adult children, have difficulty pointing the finger of responsibility at their parent or parents. They have difficulty labeling their parents or other authorities as unstable or negligent. Children are taught to love and respect their parents because they are parents; they are not instructed to evaluate or question whether their parents are deserving of that love and respect.

When Trust is Broken

Past hurtful situations have confused those with LSE; now they do not know whom or when to trust. Some become skeptical and distrustful of everyone; others in their neediness and loneliness have difficulty discerning when they can trust someone and when they should not, often making poor choices. Believing they are unworthy, children grow into adults who have difficulty trusting those who say they care, those who make commitments. Having had parents who said "I love you" while treating them in unloving ways has caused them to be suspicious. Being treated as "less than" convinces these people that they are "damaged," that they will always be inferior. When friends and loved ones try to convince them differently, they wonder; they feel patronized. The best of intentions, the most sincere compliments then fall on deaf ears.

JANE: betrayal and abuse

> *When Jane entered seventh grade, her best friend was the daughter of the local Baptist minister. The two girls often played upstairs in her friend's room, which was adjacent to the pastor's study. On one particular day when the girls were playing, Jane's friend was called downstairs by her mother for some reason; thinking her friend would be back soon, Jane stayed and continued what they had been doing. As Jane heard her friend descending the stairs, she turned to see the pastor enter the room where she was standing. He walked directly to her, wrapped his arms around her, and began trying to kiss and fondle her. Jane was terrified! She pushed against his chest as hard as she could and somehow managed to wrestle away from him. She raced down the stairs and out of the house shouting to her friend's mother that she had to go home. Thinking no one would ever believe her and that she was probably somehow to blame, she never told anyone about the incident.*

This betrayal of trust and decency by an adult authority—a minister—had a devastating effect on Jane. Though she may not have been able to articulate her feelings at the time, she was very frightened and confused afterwards. At that time and in the small community where she lived, this type of behavior was unheard of—and from a minister of all people. She felt degraded. Confused, she wondered what about her would cause him to do such a thing. After that, she was afraid to go to her friend's home and was careful never to be alone there, even for a few minutes. She became suspicious and fearful of all older men, a reaction that remained with her throughout her life.

When we do not know whom and when to trust, we set in motion the need to evaluate everything that others say or do. Needing desperately to feel loved, those of us with LSE feel compelled to determine whether or not a person's declared love is true. We do not want to foolishly trust that love and then be disappointed or hurt. We feel compelled to prove or disprove the person's loyalty, so we watch to see if our expectations are met by that person. If the person's behavior pleases us, we believe the person is trustworthy, that his love can be trusted; if he does not meet our expectations, we question his love.

Some people with LSE try to stop having expectations or lower their criteria so that the other person will be able to meet it. They settle for far less than they deserve in relationships; they may put up with abuse or other dysfunctional behaviors. Offering acceptance in hope that it will be repaid, they end up with exploiters who make them feel worse about themselves.

JANE: lost treasures

When Jane was in college, she came home one weekend to visit her mother. (Her father had died three months earlier.) After talking to her mother a few minutes, Jane went downstairs to look for the boxes she had stored there. She wanted to take her yearbooks, her scrapbooks, and other treasured books back with her now that she had her own apartment and room for them. Jane glanced around the basement but didn't see the boxes. Back upstairs, she asked her mother where her things were? Her mother replied, "Oh, the basement leaked a little this spring and some of the boxes got damp so I threw them all away." Jane couldn't believe what she was hearing, "How could you do that? Couldn't you have let them dry out? Why didn't you let me make the decision? All my yearbooks, pictures, and favorite books were in those boxes." Jane's mother just looked at Jane and said, "No, they weren't. They were just some old books

*that no one wanted." Jane felt devastated. She knew her moth-
er was lying, but there was nothing she could do. Her prized
possessions were gone. Her mother didn't even care.*

Jane's mother did not treat her with respect. She did not think
of what Jane would want, how Jane would feel. When caught in a
thoughtless and unloving act, she lied to Jane. Throughout their
relationship, Jane felt that her mother treated her as a non-person,
causing Jane to suspect that her mother did not love her. This, of
course, had a profound affect on how Jane felt about herself and
added weight to her doubts about whether anyone would ever truly
love her.

JANE: her grandmother

*Jane's father died the winter of Jane's senior year in college.
Jane spent part of that following summer at home and then
moved back into her apartment in early July to look for part-
time work before beginning graduate school. Two months later,
on a Sunday evening, Jane phoned a friend from back home
and immediately launched into a description of the job she had
found. When she finished her explanation, there was silence on
the phone. "What's wrong?" Jane asked her friend. There was
another pause and then her friend said, "Don't you know?"
"Know what?" Jane asked with apprehension. "Don't you know
your grandmother died and the funeral is tomorrow? I've been
expecting all weekend for you to call and say you were back in
town." Tears welled up in Jane's eyes, a lump formed in her
throat as quietly she repeated what she had heard, "My grandmother died?"*

*"I'm so sorry, Jane," her friend said, "I can't believe your
mother didn't call and tell you." "Can you come home tonight
or tomorrow morning? I'll go with you to the funeral." In shock*

and barely able to speak, Jane whispered, "I'll pack my bags and try to leave within an hour. It'll be late. Can I come stay with you?"

Jane and her friend finished making their plans and Jane hung up the phone. She fell on her bed and sobbed. She loved her grandmother so much and now she was dead. First her father and now her grandmother. How could her mother do this to her? How could she not call? Had her grandmother been sick? Why hadn't someone let her know? She had only been gone two months. What had happened? Jane was devastated. She could barely believe this was true. She could hardly concentrate enough to pack her suitcase.

Jane's mother did not like her mother-in-law and resented the fact that Jane always went to visit her when she was home. Throughout school and later during her weekends and summers in college, Jane had always spent a lot of time with her grandmother. In fact, Jane had seen her grandmother just before returning to school. When Jane's mother heard that her mother-in-law was ill, she did not call Jane; then even when Jane's beloved grandmother died, she did not inform her daughter. To Jane, this was the ultimate sign that her mother didn't care about her feelings, that her mother neither loved nor respected her.

We all have a profound need to be treated with consideration and respect. These are a part of love and acceptance. Knowing we are loved makes us feel acceptable and worthwhile. Experiencing approval, consideration, and acceptance makes us feel loved. Together these give us the confidence to meet life's challenges as well as the freedom and willingness to see our faults and work toward change. They give us the courage to try again when we fail. When deprived of love and acceptance, however, we are left with a deep festering wound that never fully heals.

Example:

> *A well-known sports figure, once at the top of his game, recently talked about his struggle in his early years because his father criticized him after each event; he never seemed to be good enough to please his father. Now white-haired, he emotionally told how desperately he had sought his father's approval. He went on to relate how some years later his participation was in doubt because of an injury and how concerned he was that he would have to quit. When he spoke to his father, his father replied that it really didn't matter if he couldn't play anymore. When the son asked him why that would be, the father told him, "You're already the best I've ever seen." The white-haired former athlete openly cried on television the day he shared his story as he said it was the best gift his father ever gave him. He had received his father's approval. He had finally felt fully loved and accepted.*

Obviously, this man still carried with him sadness as he recalled times of criticism and rejection by this father. And though he will never forget those early years and the pain he felt, he finally found peace in his father's words of acceptance, thereby dispelling his self-doubts. He went on to have a successful career and fulfilling life, loved and admired by many.

Unfortunately, however, this turnabout in troubled parent-child relationships is rare. In most cases, the child moves through adulthood and witnesses the death of the parent or authority figure without ever experiencing this healing period, leaving him with the emotional residue of unresolved conflict and pain.

Any attempt to repair this relationship is often left to the adult-child to initiate. Occasionally parents and adult children do make amends, restoring and rebuilding a satisfying bond; more often than not, however, the damage is never repaired and the adult-child is left to suffer the agonizing and perplexing confusion and turmoil created by the parent's negative attitude.

For the person with LSE, this struggle for self-acceptance continues until she embarks on a personal journey of self-transformation—building self-confidence and developing self-love. As she does so, a new picture of herself forms; by substituting this new evaluation of self for those flawed parental perceptions that she has adopted, she remakes her personal video. This process is much like a runner leaping over hurdles and jogging around obstacles, while striving to remain upright as she continues intact toward the finish line. At times, the uphill trek is exhausting, but the race can be won.

RECOVERY

Those of us who have lived with LSE can testify that the wounds remain as a lingering sadness in our hearts, though it lessens with time as we learn to love ourselves and be all that we can be. We can be happy; we can love and be loved. We can learn to believe in ourselves, come to accept ourselves, and learn whom to trust. We can develop solid supportive friendships. We can break the chains that have held us back and become free to discover who we are and what we want to be. It just takes time, patience, persistence, and motivation to do so.

Feelings Ignored and Devalued

In the stories of people with LSE, a common experience from their childhood is that of having their feelings ignored, devalued, or ridiculed. Feelings are our personal description of our experience in the world. When we say "I feel hurt," and the response is "You're just too sensitive," the message heard is clearly: "Our feelings don't matter!" When a child is teased or ridiculed, the message received is "What you feel is unimportant." Both of these statements are actually a form of emotional abuse.

Parents are often so focused on what they want for their children, who they want their children to be, and what they want their children to accomplish that they ignore the individual traits, needs, and abilities of each child. Without realizing it, they may push their children in ways that fulfill their own desires and dreams while totally disregarding the aspirations of their children and the right of those children to live their own dreams and set their own goals. Unaware they are doing so, parents often use their children in this way to assuage their own pain over mistakes made or opportunities lost. Unhappy with their own lives and choices, they try to compensate by taking charge of the lives of their children, as though they get to use these lives as a second chance. They give unsolicited advice, attempting to steer their children into futures that match their own preferences, not considering that the child may have totally different goals in life.

Parents also succumb to outside pressures, wanting to appear to be good parents. Without realizing it, they push their children to "look good" to the public eye, to conform to the expectations of family or community traditions while disregarding the effects on the child. In so doing, they are again actually making their own needs and feelings the priority, while ignoring the child's feelings and damaging the child's self-esteem. The child feels discounted and diminished; these pictures become a part of the video he reviews throughout his life.

When children grow to be adults, parents often continue to judge them when they make choices in sharp contrast to their own. The adult child may not conform to the parents' religious convictions, may choose alternative lifestyles, or may simply decide to become more educated or more goal-oriented than their parents were. Threatened by these choices that are so unlike their own, many parents openly ridicule and criticize, alienating their grown children; later these parents wonder why their children don't come to visit more often. Unable to separate their lives from the lives of their children, they lose out on the opportunity to relate as friends, enjoying one another and celebrating each other's uniqueness.

Unaware of the effect they are having, parents frequently withhold praise from their children, not wanting their children to become too proud or complacent. They may see criticism as a means of motivating. They may also give compliments while adding a "but" such as, "you did a good job, but...", or "I liked what you said, but..." This added "but" tends to invalidate the entire preceding compliment, turning it into a criticism. Still others treat their children as though the fact that they are children means they are devoid of feelings or that their feelings are insignificant. It may be that the old adage "Children are to be seen and not heard" is believed by these parents, or that for some other unknown reason, they only view the feelings of children as immature and selfish and, therefore, unimportant.

JANE: her trampled feelings

When Jane was a teenager, Uncle Harry and Aunt Edna came for a visit. After they arrived, Jane's mother, Linda, called to her husband and two children to come greet their guests. Jane, now 14, had never liked Uncle Harry; he frightened her. Her mother, knowing how Jane felt, insisted that she give her aunt and uncle a hug anyway. When Jane stood back, Linda, embarrassed, scolded her. Sheepishly, Jane complied with her mother's wishes but felt terrible; she did not want to hug or even touch Uncle Harry. She was angry at her mother for making her do so. She wondered why she had to hug someone she didn't like, but she knew instinctively that her mother was more concerned about Uncle Harry and Aunt Edna's feelings then she was about Jane's.

Later that day, Jane's family took Harry and Edna to dinner at a local steak house. When the young waiter came over to fill the water glasses, he accidentally dropped the half-full pitcher onto the table near Jane. She let out a quick shriek and pushed her chair back but was soaked with the icy water. Her mother shushed her because she had responded so loudly that other people were looking their way. The waiter apologized and ran off to get a towel as Linda and others at the table shoved their napkins in Jane's direction. Now Jane was both embarrassed and upset by her mother's response. Her mother patted at the water with the towel and available napkins and then said to Jane, "There, now you're all right." Jane replied, "But, Mom, I'm freezing" to which her mother responded, "Just try not to think about it; you'll dry off. Don't make a scene."

Linda was more concerned about looking good to her aunt and uncle and those in the restaurant than she was about Jane's feelings. Wanting the evening to go well with her aunt and uncle, she ignored Jane's feelings and expected Jane to do the same—to act as though everything was fine and overlook the fact that she was wet and cold. She first demanded that Jane show affection, though it did not represent her daughter's authentic feelings. Later, she expected Jane to ignore her own discomfort.

JANE: the meal

During the meal, Jane ate very little. She was humiliated and angry. Her mother encouraged her to eat, saying, "Aren't you hungry, honey? Is something wrong with your steak? Don't you like your salad?" Jane shook her head. She felt close to tears. Why was her mother acting as though nothing was wrong, she wondered. Why was she treating her as though she was the one who had made a mistake?

After a while, Linda became frustrated with her sullen daughter, who was only picking at her food. She leaned over to Jane and said, "Don't be this way, Jane. Just get over it so we can all have a good time." Jane was further devastated by her mother's words.

Later when they were getting ready to leave, Jane leaned across the table toward her father and said, "You're not going to leave them a tip, are you? After what happened to me?" Linda, hearing her daughter's words, looked at her husband and quietly said, "Of course, we need to leave a tip." Then to Jane she said, "Just forget about it, Jane. You're making too much of this."

Jane was very depressed when the day was over. She knew she had disappointed her mother. She also felt enraged with her mother but was confused about whether her anger was justified. What was she supposed to have done, she wondered? What was right in this situation? Linda's words seemed to pass judgment on Jane, yet she couldn't understand what was wrong with her behavior. She felt like her mother just didn't care about her or her feelings. Obviously it just hadn't mattered that she had had to sit through the meal in wet clothes.

The Anger-Guilt Cycle

When adult children with LSE continue to receive criticism and disapproval from a parent, they are extremely hurt, then angry; many become enraged. Feeling discounted and not knowing what to do, they want to distance from the person who has hurt them, possibly vowing not to return or see them again. They have hateful thoughts toward the parent. Later, they start to feel guilty because they believe they should honor and love their parents, no matter what. Wanting desperately to have a loving relationship with the parent, they chastise themselves; they convince themselves that they should be more patient, more forgiving, more loving toward the parent. They may even believe that they have somehow triggered the parent's behavior. They begin to think that the next time will be different, maybe they just overreacted. Surely their parent didn't mean to be so cruel.

With that in mind, the person with LSE again initiates spending time with the parent. Of course, the parent is who he/she is and the unaccepting and critical behavior is repeated. The adult child is again devastated; once again he becomes furious. He escapes as soon as possible and may become depressed. He ruminates about the situation for hours, days, even weeks, eventually feeling guilty once again. He makes a plan to spend time with the parent or abusive adult, determining to alter the interactive pattern they have established. He visits again and the cycle continues.

The anger-guilt cycle is common. Parent-child relationships are very complex; those who find themselves in this cycle may repeat it for decades. They may try to think of what they can do differently, trying to come up with a strategy that will make their next time with the parent more fulfilling. They may try to ignore their own feelings, make excuses for a particular statement or response of the parent, or even believe that they themselves are really to blame. Nothing they do will achieve what they want, for they do not have the power to change their parent.

Only if and when adult children can point their fingers at the true problem—the parent, can they find release from the chains of the anger-guilt cycle. Only when they can face the fact that the parent is at fault, that the parent is the perpetrator of this problem, can they see the situation accurately. For, we should be angry when we are mistreated; verbal and emotional abuse is never acceptable. We should want to stay away from people who are cruel. We have every right to feel hurt by those who are disparaging.

With this recognition comes freedom. It may come in the form of freedom to be assertive with the parent, confronting the inappropriate behavior, or it may come in the freedom to realize that we do not have to continue to place ourselves in a position to be criticized or ridiculed but that we can protect ourselves instead. We can stay away or at least limit our contact. This option, of course, is not available to younger children who may experience this cycle thousands of times while growing up.

Everyone is lovable

In truth, all people are lovable. That does not mean, of course, that everyone will love us or that we will love everyone else but there are people who can really love us just as we will meet people we will grow to love. When we can understand and separate the facts about who we are from inappropriate and inaccurate feedback about us, we can begin to find our true selves. Sorting out these feelings is a difficult task and one that requires help, whether from a loved one or a therapist. It also takes time.

The process of healing requires that we be willing to examine our backgrounds, recognizing and understanding what has been done to us that has caused us to have self-doubts. We need to be willing to sort out who was to blame, an exercise that many of us shy away from. We do not believe we should blame our past for our present attitudes and behaviors, yet the truth is that until we do understand our pasts, we will only reflect what we learned there. As we come to grips with the dynamics of our early years, we can begin to understand the deficiencies in our parents or other authority figures that have left us feeling unworthy; we can begin to recognize the impact that circumstances have played in our present view of ourselves. Then, and only then, can we begin to distance ourselves from this feedback, challenging its authenticity. Only then can we make choices and set goals that are uniquely our own. Only then can we free ourselves from the burden of dysfunction and break the chain of low self-esteem that we drag around and that impedes our progress.

• *A note of comparison with those with healthy self-esteem:*

People with healthy self-esteem feel loved and love themselves. They know they are lovable and may never have even questioned the fact; consequently, they are not faced with these struggles.

Those who experience consistent healthy self-esteem are likely the products of positive and uplifting environments. They probably have good familial relationships and interactions and regularly receive encouragement and support from family members.

They are trusting but streetwise; generally able to discern who and when to trust, they also recognize it takes time to determine how trustworthy or dependable others are. They are not needy, and so they have no reason to confide in others immediately. They have support systems and people who care for them, so they do not need the instant gratification of jumping too quickly into a new relationship.

RECOVERY

The struggle to believe in ourselves, to believe we are lovable, is at the heart of the battle to overcome LSE. To accomplish this awesome task, we have to be willing to look at our past and determine who the significant people were and what the critical events were that shaped our self-doubts. As with Jane, we see that her mother largely shaped her view of herself. If we were to analyze this situation objectively, we would undoubtedly realize that Jane's mother had her own problems—maybe she also had low self-esteem. We would then try to understand her actions and their validity based on seeing her as an unhealthy person herself. With this in mind, we might begin to see that her evaluations, her actions toward Jane did not reflect the truth but were signs of her own feelings of inadequacy. Eventually, we might be able to see how Jane could begin to distance herself somewhat from those hurtful events, recognizing that they did not represent the truth about her but rather the truth about her mother or any other authority figures whose responses so pervaded her process of self-examination. As in any battle, the going is rough, and at times victory may not seem attainable; through perseverance, however, while keeping our eyes on the goal, we can triumph over this vicious enemy—low self-esteem.

THINGS TO DO

We each have an obligation to take care of ourselves. Part of that responsibility is to consider our feelings and emotional well-being as important enough to protect from harm. When others treat us in ways that are injurious, we have a duty to extricate ourselves from those people. This is difficult, of course, if the person is a family member; it may be necessary to try another approach such as the one below.

If there is a person in your life that you feel continuously triggers your feelings of inadequacy, incompetence, or unworthiness, but this person is someone important that you do not want to totally eliminate from your life, consider the following suggestions.

1. Attempt to set personal boundaries by limiting the frequency of visits or times you agree to get together with this person.

2. Limit the amount of time spent with this person on the occasions you do see him or her. You may do this by visiting at times when you have another appointment following your stay.

3. Try to spend time with this person engaged in an activity like attending a movie, school play, or musical event that requires less interaction than many other situations.

In Chapter 9, we will discuss assertive communication that you may eventually be able to implement; until then, you should not expose yourself to more negative feedback than you feel is absolutely necessary. These suggestions are only a beginning, but they may structure your time with the person more constructively.

8

The Relentless
Pursuit of Validation

JANE: wanting to feel special to someone

When she began spending time with her new friend Harriet, Jane was concerned whether the relationship would last. Questioning her own worthiness, she continued to wonder why Harriet would want to be her friend. She liked and admired Harriet's enthusiasm, ambition, and sense of humor, but what did she have to offer Harriet?

Though Harriet had taken the lead by first suggesting they get together and had continued to initiate activities and regular phone contact, Jane worried that Harriet might tire of her. When over the weeks and months their time spent together increased, Jane still questioned why, if, and how much Harriet cared about her. In an attempt to squelch her anxiety, she consciously noted how often Harriet initiated activities, how often she called, and she watched to see if Harriet spent as much time with her as she spent with other friends.

Jane wanted to feel that she was special to Harriet, wanted to feel that Harriet liked her best. Desperately needing this validation, Jane actually made a plan she thought would confirm or refute Harriet's loyalty and feelings for her. Knowing that Harriet usually went walking every Saturday morning with another friend, Jane asked Harriet to join her in an activity the following Saturday, an activity that would take place at the same time as her regularly scheduled walk. She thought that if Harriet was willing to cancel her plans with her other friend, this would prove that Harriet indeed liked her best.

The Set-up and Testing

The person with activated LSE has difficulty knowing whom to trust and when to trust. Jane's mother never told Jane she loved her although she sent her effusive cards on special occasions and would surely have said she loved Jane if asked. At the same time, however, she was emotionally abusive to Jane. How could Jane believe these written expressions of love when she didn't see them in action? Jane thought parents were "supposed" to love their children, yet what she experienced seemed anything but loving.

All of us would be suspicious and doubtful in these circumstances. Like Jane, we might then be confused and have difficulty believing anyone else who says he loves us. We would be on guard, looking for signs that would confirm if the other person's behavior was consistent with his commitment or declaration of love. We would feel compelled to know the truth; we would not want to become complacent, trusting blindly and then be hurt. Without being aware we were doing so, those of us with LSE might "set a trap" to check out our suspicions, hoping this set-up would allay our fears and assure us about the relationship.

The set-up and testing begins when a person who is questioning the devotion of another person forms a specific plan (the set-up) to find out if his doubts are true. To do this, he consciously makes a mental list of expectations for a future event. When the time comes for the situation to take place, he then watches closely to see if his expectations are met. This is the "test." If his expectations are met, he is temporarily satisfied and believes the person must love him. If they are not, he is upset, believing this means the person does not love him.

Figure 5: Two Extremes in Relating

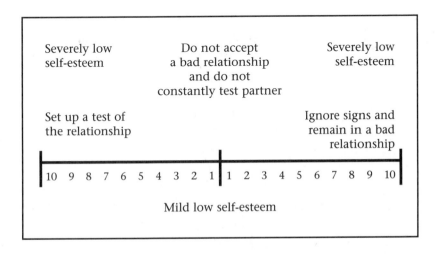

Additionally, the person with LSE decides that if his partner will do certain things for him, her actions prove her love. These expectations become very specific as he looks for the slightest inconsistencies that demonstrate her lack of love. This is another test. Many people with severe LSE test their partners; others purposely avoid tests and overlook their partner's behavior because they do not want to face the truth about a bad relationship. (See Figure 4 above.) Both are equally dysfunctional and another example of how those with low self-esteem tend to respond in opposite and extreme ways.

The following are ways in which those with low self-esteem "set up" another person to be tested. What is usually being tested is whether the other person cares and how much. The LSE sufferer:

- Performs specific, well-planned behaviors or actions as a test.

    Examples:

    1. Fixes a special dinner, buys a little surprise, or does some thing special for a person. Later, the person watches and waits to see if her partner will do something similar in return, which would indicate he loves her.

    2. Wears a particular item of clothing to see if her partner notices and comments. If he fails to comment on her clothes, he will have failed the test.

    3. Makes flattering remarks to her significant other about a handsome available man whom they both know to see if it will make him jealous. If he doesn't show signs of jealousy, he will have failed the test.

- Uses specific questions to assess the devotion of a loved one.

    Examples:

    1. Requesting that the person do a specific task, chore, or errand at a specific time, to see if she cares enough to do it and to do it at the exact time requested.

    2. Asking the person to buy something expensive that will stretch her financial resources, to see how much she cares.

    3. Asking the person questions that require she compare their current relationship to her past ones (e.g., "Am I as

much fun as he was?" or "Did he take you out to nice places like I do?" or "How was the sex with him?"

4. Requesting that the person spend time with him when he knows she is exceptionally busy to see how much he values time with her.

- Purposely refrains from mentioning plans they have made or activities that are coming up to see if he remembers. If he doesn't, she concludes he doesn't care.

Examples:

1. Refrains from mentioning upcoming dinner plans to see if he remember. If he doesn't she concludes he doesn't care.

2. Avoids mentioning the important meeting she had that day, to see if he cares enough to remember and ask about it.

3. Purposely doesn't mention a recent injury to see if he cares enough to ask about it.

4. Consciously refrains from initiating sex to see if he is interested enough to do so.

- Solicits specific feedback.

Examples:

1. Asks specific questions, fishes for compliments, to see how effusive he will be.

2. Tells the significant other she loves him to see if he will say it back.

- Watches to see if expectations are met.

Examples:

1. Does he follow through on commitments like doing his chores when he said he would?

2. Does he show up when he said he would?

3. Does he call at the exact time he said he would?

It is important to recognize and remember that each of these tests has a distinct purpose. With LSE, we feel vulnerable and inadequate. We are unable to trust that we are truly loved; we fear looking like a fool. To check out our perceptions, we set up both ourselves and the other by administering a series of tests designed to either give credence to our doubts or to squelch them.

The person with LSE does this on automatic pilot. He is unaware that he is maneuvering in a way that others do not. To him, it seems normal and even wise to check out his perceptions, especially considering that he has often been wrong in the past about knowing whom and when to trust. It seems perfectly logical. Where he wanders from a healthy plan, however, is in his chosen techniques for discerning the truth: he believes that his expectations of others are normal and appropriate when they are not. His unrealistic expectations require perfection from others and do not allow for basic human error or separate agendas.

When testing others, the person with LSE has no idea she is also sabotaging herself. She is merely looking for a way to feel better about the relationship and to feel valued as a person. She is not aware that anyone really searching for a reason to distrust can ultimately find some hook on which to hang her hat. She does not allow for the busyness of life, expecting others to be focused only on her and her needs. Thus, what she often sees as disinterest or neglect are the signs of preoccupation with other tasks and attention to other details of daily living.

Following the disappointing but expected failure of friend, mate, or family member, the person with LSE experiences a self-esteem attack, feeling humiliated, disillusioned, and devastated. His worst suspicions have now been confirmed: he is unloved, maybe unlovable. He falls into his habitual response as either a Noisy or Quiet Reactor.

The person who is the target of the test never knows until she has failed that the exam was taking place. Not until she witnesses the devastation, anger, or withdrawal of the tester will she know something is askew in the relationship. When presented with her failure (as evidenced by her lack of appreciation, affection, commitment, or action), she will be dumbfounded, unaware of what she has done and what this means to her partner. She may never know, in fact, because he may never tell her, assuming that it would be obvious to "any decent person." If he does explain her shortcomings, she will be perplexed but may try to please or may become defensive. When this behavior becomes a pattern, she will become frustrated and irritated, and she, too, will become ambivalent about the relationship.

Another self-sabotaging behavior of the person with LSE is that of altering her expectations so that they become more precise over time. Thus, if a partner who realizes he has failed to meet an expectation tries to comply with that expectation at a later time, he may still fail because the expectation has been slightly altered—another test. For instance, the person with LSE may set up this test: "If he really loves me, he will offer to get the groceries today even though it's my job, because he knows how busy I am." Recognizing this issue as one that has come up before, the partner offers to get the groceries. He takes the list, makes the purchases, and returns home. Later she is upset and says, "It would have been nice if you had added some special treat." To herself she thinks, "He would have, if he really loved me." The partner begins to feel like a blind mouse running through a maze.

Couples who repeatedly experience this pattern eventually get very discouraged by the misunderstandings, confrontations, and doubts of the one who struggles with low self-esteem. This problem, however, can be dealt with, though often not without outside help. What the person with LSE needs is someone who can explain these destructive patterns and excessive expectations, as often as necessary, until the doubting person can see the irrationality of his behavior. This often requires a third person, however, because the one with LSE is already suspicious and will not take the word of his partner, concerned that it may be a form of manipulation. When the person with LSE experiences the respectful assistance from a trained and objective bystander, he can eventually understand and correct his thinking and his behavior. Couples who then work together, are thrilled about the change this brings to their relationship.

In many cases where the partner of an LSE sufferer is quick to praise and tell his partner he loves her, that person may have complete trust and feel fully secure in their relationship even though she has trouble knowing whom and when to trust outside the relationship. She may feel fully confident and feel good about herself in the relationship because he is unwavering in his devotion, while she remains filled with self-doubt in other areas of her life. Thus, having a warm and loving relationship can dissolve the fear of distrust for the LSE sufferer, at least in that one close connection where she feels fully accepted and supported.

Counting Behaviors

Another part of testing is watching for the frequency of specific key words or actions in others—in other words, counting behaviors. One of the ways the person with LSE tries to determine the commitment of her significant other is to actually count the number of times the partner does or says certain things. For instance, she may feel that "if" he really loves her, he will say "I love you" a certain number of times or at specific moments, maybe daily or following an act of kindness on her part. She then watches and "keeps score," tabulating the frequency of these endearing statements. When he does not say or do what she expects according to her unspoken schedule, she feels rejected.

Yet another form of testing is to say a phrase with the expectation that a certain phrase will be returned, e.g., "I missed you today" waiting to see if the partner responds similarly, then remaining aware of how often this happens. The test may be that she asks him to make choices that show she is loved more than another friend, his pet, his computer, or even the newspaper. For instance, the person with LSE may count how many times her partner chooses to spend time with her in the evenings instead of working on his computer or she may ask him to do a chore and tally the times when he follows through. The tests are endless; however, it is important to realize that she is unaware she is doing anything abnormal or self-destructive. She unknowingly designs these tests so the person will inevitably fail, and she always remembers the scores. From her perspective, the test is valid and the results are trustworthy.

Of course, what the person with LSE wants is to be proven wrong—to be shown beyond a shadow of a doubt that he is truly loved, that he is indeed lovable. However, experience has shown that the times he let his guard down in the past, he was sorely mistaken. He does not wish to go through that pain again. What he does not realize is that he is creating his own pain through his hypervigilance and excessive demands on others.

The following is a list of typical counting behaviors:

- Tracking the frequency of gifts given to us

- Remembering the dollar amount others spend on our gifts

- Deciding how much effort others have gone to in purchasing our gifts

- Adding up the amount of time others spend with us, as compared to time they spend with others

- Tallying the number of compliments someone gives us

- Remembering the number of times someone initiates contact with us

- Totaling the number of times someone calls us

- Computing how much time and energy the other person puts into the relationship with us

- Comparing how much attention someone gives us with how much he gives others

- Remembering how often others apologize when we think they should

- Counting the number of times the other person offers to pay when out together

- Tallying the number of times others offer to help us with projects

- Tracking how often others remember significant days in our lives

- Remembering the number of times others invite us to their home

Those with low self-esteem go to great lengths to compare how people treat them vs. how they treat others; they feel very insecure if they think they are receiving less attention and energy. They also listen to stories of their partner's previous relationships, evaluating these stories in the same way. At times, some LSE sufferers may purposely refrain from calling someone, waiting to see if the other person calls first. They may do something for another person just to see if the other person reciprocates. They may flirt or be overly attentive to others to see if their partners become jealous. Life becomes one big test.

It is important to mention again that people with LSE do not act in these self-defeating ways at all times. For days, weeks, or even years, they are busily occupied with the normal demands of life, feeling relatively good about themselves and acting like others around them. They are not "testing," "setting anyone up," or "counting." They are hard-working people with careers; many of them are highly successful. Then, without warning, something happens to trigger a self-esteem attack: they lose a loved one, suffer an occupational setback, or experience some other perceived failure. As a result, they become deeply depressed or even despairing, a state in which they remain for a short or long period of time. If the trigger was related to a relationship, they may feel vulnerable and begin doubting the relationship; at this point, the "testing" will begin. Even a small negative statement or minor inconsiderate act can be enough to start the process.

Scenarios

Scenarios are stories those of us with LSE write in our heads to confirm that someone is treating us badly; these scenarios justify our suspicions and anger. For instance, when we are disappointed by the actions of a significant person in our lives, we begin "watching" reruns of all the other times they've hurt us; we are highly suspicious. We use our memories along with our excessive expectations to weave a story that proves our irrational position, a process so automatic we are usually unaware we are doing it. It is a means by which we accuse the culprit, put together an airtight case, then convict and sentence him—all without his knowledge.

Example:

Mel, who has low self-esteem, announces to his partner, Dan, that he is planning to work in the garden on Saturday. He assumes that Dan will volunteer to work along with him, knowing Mel wants and needs his help. Mel waits for him to offer. (This is the set-up—Dan's commitment to him is about to be tested.)

Two days later, Dan comes home and states he will be working Saturday as his boss has offered him some overtime. He doesn't even mention the garden. Mel is upset and feels rejected. (Dan has failed the unannounced test.)

An argument ensues in which Mel is angry and accusing. Dan is amazed that Mel expects him to be involved in his project when he hadn't asked him. He is also bewildered because it is Mel's garden and Dan had made it clear when Mel planted it that he hated gardening.

As the argument continues, Mel begins to build his case. He convinces himself that Dan:

- *Was well aware that he needed and expected assistance in the garden.*

- *Purposely took on the extra work so as not to be available to help him.*

- *Is not as committed to the relationship as he is.*

- *Has disappointed him in similar ways in the past.*

- *Has always cared more about his work than about Mel.*

- *Purposely waited until Friday night to tell Mel just to make it more hurtful.*

Mel may even later conclude that Dan has never really loved him, feeling embarrassed and foolish to think that he has been duped. He may continue scenario-building and ruminating for hours or days, dredging up even more memories of Dan's hurtful actions. This may lead to more chaotic confrontations. Eventually, however, something will happen to "snap" Mel out of it—a kind word or some show of affection from Dan or some realization that he probably overreacted. (As Mel becomes more aware of his self-esteem problems, he will be able to recognize his self-defeating behaviors before they become full-blown and then will be able to alter them.)

Scenario-building is damaging to a relationship because these made-up stories contain just enough truth to justify the irrational person's conclusions but also so many distortions that the findings are far from accurate. Mel may have many justifiable complaints about Dan, but taken out of context, they are magnified and twisted to such proportions that they cannot be resolved, leaving the entire relationship in question. Mixed with his ever-present self-doubts, Mel may decide that this relationship has never been a good one; once again, he feels a fool to have trusted and given so much of himself to an unreliable and insensitive person, as Dan most surely is.

Scenarios maintain and fuel the irrationality of the person with LSE. They continually erode and destroy trust, wedging themselves between the two individuals and forming a brick wall. It is important to remember that the individual suffering from LSE does not do this on purpose, nor does she receive anything from the process but pain. She is merely trying to protect herself from making a mistake and looking foolish; she has a deep-seated fear of abandonment and wants to be forewarned if she is likely to be left behind again. These and other fears are constantly lurking nearby and seem to pounce upon her whenever she is vulnerable.

Hidden Agendas

People with LSE form hidden agendas, specific expectations of others that are unannounced and that will, therefore, go unmet. Our assuming that others share these agendas (negating any need to mention them) make them exactly what their name implies: hidden or unspoken. Because others are unaware these expectations exist, they will be unable to meet them, leaving those with LSE hurt and disillusioned about the relationship.

Because of the existence of an internal rule book and the wrong assumption that others have a similar set of rules, those with LSE expect others to know what they want, what they need, and when they need it. They expect their partners to know they need affection at a specific time, know they need help with a project, or know they want to go out to dinner. They wrongly assume that if they have to ask or tell someone what they want, the other will only respond out of duty rather than making an effort to please on his own. To the person with LSE, this diminishes the effect of the results. They tend to believe that "if you loved me, you would antiicpate my needs. If I have to prompt you, the action is meaningless."

Example:

Matthew and Janette have been married three years, a relationship that has not been totally satisfying to Janette. She feels Matt is not as attentive or supportive as she needs him to be, and they have quarreled about this many times. Janette struggles with bouts of low self-esteem and feels that her relationship has added to her negative feelings about herself. She wonders if Matt really loves her. She fantasizes about what he could do to prove this to her—what would make her feel secure. "If he would just throw me a big surprise birthday party for my 30th birthday next month—that would do it," she thinks. She decides to throw some hints to Matt, ones he can't possibly miss.

Systematically, Janette begins her plan. Nearly once a day she says something to Matt about birthdays and birthday parties, stressing how much she likes surprise birthday parties, how fun she thought the surprise party had been for Matt's mother last year; she talks to him about how amazing it is that she will soon be 30 years old. When two weeks before her birthday, Matt announces that she needs to keep her birthday weekend free, she knows he is planning her party. She is elated. "He really does care," she tells herself. She starts imagining who he is inviting. She wonders where he will order the cake and if he will actually decorate the house. She vows to stay out of his way as much as possible so he will think it really is a surprise.

As the days go by, Janette hears Matt on the phone and avoids going into the room, assuming he is talking to someone about her party. This doesn't happen very often, however, but she figures he is making most of his calls from work. Without being too obvious, she cleans the house when Matt is gone so it will be presentable for guests—and the party.

On Wednesday evening before her birthday, Matt approaches her, "Guess I'd better tell you that I'm taking you to the beach Friday afternoon. I know how much you like the beach and thought it would be a fun way to spend your birthday." "That's great, honey," Janette responds. To herself she says, "So, the surprise party must be Saturday evening when we get back. That's pretty sneaky of him. Our friends must be coming over to decorate while we're gone!"

Friday they drive to the beach and have a fun afternoon. Matt has flowers waiting in their room and has even made dinner reservations. Janette has a wonderful time, all the while anticipating the party that will be waiting when they get back. "Matt really has outdone himself for her birthday," she tells herself.

Saturday afternoon Matt is in no hurry to return to the city. By 5:30, knowing they have a two-hour drive ahead of them, Janette says to him, "Shouldn't we be starting for home?" "What's the hurry?" Matt replies. "He's a sly one," Janette thinks, but says, "I just think it will be nice to get home and enjoy the evening together." Matt studies her since she usually wants to stay as long as they can and then agrees. They walk back down the beach toward their car and start for home.

As they near their house, Janette begins to get excited. Driving into their driveway, she unobtrusively looks for familiar cars on the street but knows her friends are too smart and will have parked around the block. The house is dark and Janette imagines people hiding behind the living room furniture and in the kitchen waiting for them to open the front door. She chuckles to herself. Matt suggests she go on in and he will bring the luggage, but Janette says she will wait for him so they can go in together—she wants him to enjoy the moment. Holding the purchases they made at the beach, Janette leads the way up the front steps and gets her key ready to open the door. Matt is right behind her with the luggage in both hands.

Janette turns the key in the lock and places her hand on the door knob, taking a big breath. She steps in and reaches for the light switch. It is so quiet. She flicks the switch and stands perfectly still—there isn't a sound. She looks around—there aren't any decorations. There is no cake. There are no people. There is no party. Janette comes out of her daze to realize that Matt is talking, urging her to step on in so he can get past her with the suitcases.

Badly shaken, Janette barely shuffles out of his way. He glances around at her and asks her if something is wrong. She just stares at him. He didn't plan a party for her, she realizes. He doesn't really love her. He even purposely misled her. She is devastated.

Hidden agendas usually remain hidden until the other person fails to meet the expectation, after which the person with LSE expresses his disappointment and resentment or withdraws (depending on whether he is a Quiet or Noisy Reactor). Both types frequently complain about how indifferent or insensitive someone is. Noisy Reactors are more likely to do so aggressively while Quiet Reactors may resort to passive-aggressive tactics. (More on this in Chapter 9.)

Those with LSE also become preoccupied with what the person's behavior means. Those in therapy bombard their counselors with questions like "What do you think he meant when he said. . .?" or "Why do you think she. . .?" as though the therapist might know. They would like a positive and rational explanation that might dispel their fears, but they are often unwilling to accept such clarification when it is given. Suspicious, they continue to put a negative "spin" on the situation and are usually left believing the worst case scenario—"He just doesn't care."

To have expectations of others is normal; we could not live without them. However, the expectations of people with severely low self-esteem are excessive in the following ways:

- Frequency—those of us with LSE constantly have expectations of others around us—mostly unspoken.

- Specificity—the expectations of those of us with LSE are extremely specific. If the expectation is not met in exactly the right way, with exactly the right words, in the right tone of voice and at the right time, we are greatly disappointed.

- Assumption—Those of us with LSE presume others think just like we do or can read our minds. Others "should know" what we expect without it being stated.

- *A note of comparison with those with healthy self-esteem:*

Healthy people do not engage in counting behaviors, scenario building, or set-ups and testing. Those with healthy self-esteem may at times have hidden agendas, but these stem from a failure to communicate their thoughts rather than distrust and a need to test someone's love. Their expectations may also be due to specific family rituals or traditions they experienced in their past that they assume are common to others: If they have been raised in a community or family that regularly enjoyed picnicking, for example, they may expect that others enjoy this too. If they were raised in an affluent home, they may think that they will always take lavish vacations. If they grew up in a small Midwest community where everyone knows and visits with their neighbors, they may move to the city expecting their neighbors to be equally friendly. If they frequently saw their parents show affection to one another in front of the children or were disciplined in certain ways, they may expect their partner to be comfortable with this as well. These differences, however, are soon recognized by the couple and discussed until each understands the other's position. Neither assumes that the other is purposefully withholding affection or cooperation, nor do they assume their partner's behavior indicates a lack of love.

Unequal Partners

When it comes to selecting friends and potential partners, those with LSE who have not dealt with their issues frequently choose individuals who are even more unhealthy than they are themselves. Unknowingly they are drawn to those who are needy, in part because such people are more available and, on the surface at least, more accepting. This is also less threatening than attempting to build a relationship with an "equal" who may be out of reach, or an even healthier individual who may recognize our flaws and issues.

In addition, if we do begin a relationship with a healthier person, she may want to take the relationship more slowly, which is threatening to those with LSE; we tend to view her as dragging her feet, a sure sign of rejection. Or as the healthier person tries to balance this relationship with separate friends and interests, those with LSE may become more dependent, even desperate. Each action the other takes is interpreted personally, almost defensively, by those with LSE, as though the need of the other to remain independent is a criticism of us.

People with LSE also choose people "to take care of," people who, they think, "need them." They hope they can find love by proving themselves indispensable. They are too threatened to choose those they consider above them, so they select people who have less experience, less money, fewer resources, fewer friends, or less education so they will not feel inferior. Women with LSE often choose "needy" men; men with LSE often choose "dependent, compliant" women. Both then feel more secure because they feel needed; they translate that into being loved.

In choosing needy people to relate to, those with LSE may enter into relationships with people who are selfish and critical, people whose lives are filled with crises and turmoil, people who saturate the environment with negativity and chaos, the exact opposite of what any of us, but especially those of us with LSE, need.

When LSE sufferers do find a truly healthy partner, they often succeed in pushing that person away while testing their love because they have difficulty believing such a wonderful person could really love them. Having learned not to trust words, they find it hard to accept the warmth, love, and affection that is offered to them, thus continuing the pattern of self-sabotage.

• *A note of comparison with those with healthy self-esteem:*

Healthy people choose healthy partners. They do not build their relationships out of a sense of needing someone to make them feel whole. Instead, they involve themselves with interesting, growing, open, and stable people who embrace similar values and whose companionship further enhances their already fulfilling lives. They desire independence and value that same quality in others. They do not look for people to "fix" nor do they expect someone to take care of them. They want to relate to those they see as equals.

RECOVERY

From what you have read to this point, you are now aware of how vulnerable and needy LSE sufferers are. You can understand their pain, if not first-hand, then by what you have read here. You see the complexity of their struggles, the difficulty trusting themselves or others, the confusion over what to do or not to do, the desire to do what is appropriate without knowing how that would look. You realize the inner turmoil they experience—constantly fearful of making a mistake or being rejected—and how difficult they find everyday life to be. And now you see some of the mistakes they make in trying to control their surroundings so that they will not do something that will make them feel even worse about themselves. Constantly on guard to the possibility that someone might be taking advantage of them, they become so hypersensitive and so hypervigilant that they analyze every behavior and word of their partners and friends. And of course, as has already been mentioned, if we look hard enough, we can usually find something that supports our foregone conclusion

Consequently, those with LSE must first become aware of their dysfunctional behavior. They must begin to see that what they are doing is having the opposite effect of what they are striving for; that their attempts to provide security for themselves by watching for inconsistencies in their partners' behaviors only produce more insecurity as they irrationally hone in on one particular behavior at a time and misjudge its meaning for the relationship. The previous pages point out how obsessed LSE sufferers can get in the pursuit of validation—they are relentless! These pages also demonstrate how self-defeating the behaviors of those who have severely low self-esteem are.

Going through a process of recovery is the only answer. Again, this won't happen overnight—for you cannot remove a learned habit or way of thinking that you have engaged in all your life quickly. Instead, recovery is a step-by-step process requiring that you first becoming aware of your distorted thinking and second that you gain awareness of the specific ways you are sabotaging yourself. Next comes the process of making changes by replacing distorted thoughts with those based on truth, fact, or history, and next by gradually altering the behaviors that accompany this distorted thinking. Most people are unable to do this on their own but need guidance, at least in the beginning, as they cannot recognize the dysfunction in the behaviors that they have practiced for so long. But be hopeful! Recovery is possible!

THINGS TO DO

Exercise 1

If you are aware that you have excessive expectations, you are well on your way to getting rid of them. Remember, getting to that awareness is a gigantic step in recovering from this pattern of self-destructive behavior. As you try to stop this behavior, do the following:

1. Tell yourself you are not going to "play games" in your relationships. Remind yourself of this whenever you start ruminating about the other person's behavior or questioning his devotion.

2. Decide that you will take the risk in relationships to ask for what you want. Be specific— don't expect another person to know what's in your mind.

3. Decide that you will take the risk in your relationships to say what you feel. Try to expect the best of the other person. Tell yourself he is truly interested in your feelings but can't be aware of them if they go unspoken. If you find this isn't true— he doesn't care about your feelings—think seriously of detaching yourself from this relationship.

4. If possible, check your perceptions out with a friend, confidant, or your therapist. Don't assume that all of your expectations are bad or inappropriate. You may, in fact, be in a bad relationship and have perfectly realistic expectations.

5. Try not to keep score. Remember we are all the sum totals of our pasts; we each think differently depending on the specifics of that past. Be willing to tell the person what you would like them to do.

6. Be willing to discuss your expectations. Try to trust that the person is equally interested in meeting your needs when reasonable.

7. Refrain from beating yourself up when you realize you have overreacted. It's not your fault you have LSE. Keep trying; you'll get there.

This new thinking pattern will need to be repeated again and again until you have reprogrammed yourself to be open and honest with the person involved. In time, you will be able to recognize when your tendency is to "test" the other person, and you will be able to stop yourself from doing so.

THINGS TO DO

Exercise 2

It is important to be aware of the kind of people we choose to be involved with. Are they needy people who suck dry our emotional resources? Are they people who trigger our LSE because they, too, have considerable emotional baggage? Are they people who encourage us and desire what is best for us? Do they engage in side-by-side, equal relationships or do they encourage relationships that have a hierarchical component?

1. Make a list of the significant people in your life.

2. On another piece of paper make two columns, one marked Positive and the other marked Negative.

3. Think about each person on your list. Ask yourself: Is this person supportive, encouraging and accepting of you? of your ideas? of your choices? Is this person communicative, open to discussing and resolving issues? Do you feel better about yourself when you are with this person? If so, this person is a "positive" influence in your life. Place that person's name in the Positive column.

   Ask yourself: Is this person critical and negative, generally putting you down? rude or sarcastic? unaccepting of you? Does he ignore your feelings? Do you tend to feel anxious or upset after spending time with this person? If so, this person is a "negative" influence in your life. Place this name in the Negative column. (This is not a license, of course, to discount the feedback of someone who points out obvious inappropriate behavior, like excessive drinking, eating disorders, or drug abuse. Be willing to take a look at your life if there is consistent negative feedback about a particular behavior or set of behaviors that may need correcting.)

4. Determine to surround yourself with positive, accepting people. Most people who have LSE come from environments that were negative or critical and we were powerless to change those circumstances. Now as adults we have a choice about who we associate with, who we spend time with. We no longer need to be regularly subjected to influences that are painful. To find that you are in such a relationship is very sad, but to remain in it is tragic.

5. Look at your list. Are there people on your list who do not enhance your life? Are there people on your list who do not encourage your growth? Are there people on your list who do not respect your feelings? Circle these names.

6. Make a plan to eliminate from your life those people who do not support you in your endeavors.

   a. If this is a person you do not work with or live near, then do not call or initiate activity with them. If they require an explanation for your behavior change, you can either choose to be assertive and explain how you feel or if you are unable to do so at this point, simply be busy and unavailable to spend time with them.

   b. If this is a person you work with, confine your communication to work-related issues or small talk. Do not initiate conversation about your personal life or theirs. Plan activities following work that make you unavailable. Be friendly but aloof.

   c. If this is a family member, try limiting the frequency and length of your visits. Avoid asking for advice or sharing information that is personal or of a sensitive nature, or information that reveals your ideas, plans, opinions, and feelings.

Decide as you build new relationships in the future to take notice of the effects that each relationship has on your self-esteem and your emotional well being—decide that you will not continue in a relationship that continually drags you down or causes you to question your adequacy and self-worth.

9

Altering the Patterns of Low Self-Esteem

JANE: responding to a self-esteem attack

After she and John divorced, Jane went through several years of reoccurring depression. When her brooding continued, she finally contacted an old friend who prodded her until she entered therapy. There, she began to have insights into her self-sabotaging behaviors. Thinking back about the many arguments she and John had endured, she began to recognize a pattern in the way she had responded to these and other negative interactions in her life—a very familiar pattern—and one her therapist said could be changed. Her therapist asked her to explain in detail an experience in which she had become depressed or devastated and Jane told the following story:

When Jane had been dating a fellow named Eric regularly for nearly three months, they were out to dinner one evening. Stacy, a woman Jane had known since high school, entered the restaurant. Jane and Stacy had often spent time together but had lost contact after Jane's marriage and subsequent divorce; they were excited to see each other and animated conversation filled the air. After a few minutes, Eric glanced at Jane with *raised eyebrows and when she nodded asked if Stacy would like to join them. Stacy plunked herself down at their table.*

As the evening progressed, Jane thought Stacy seemed quite taken with Eric; though speaking to Jane, she was often looking at him. Jane thought Stacy was flirting with him. She wondered why Eric wasn't doing something to discourage her; instead, he seemed to be enjoying the attention. Jane was hurt and frightened. By the time dessert came, Stacy and Eric were involved in a lively discussion about her work; though they made eye contact with her, Jane felt left out and unable to join in. As she continued to feel more and more excluded, she quietly withdrew into herself. Finally, feeling humiliated and tearful, she excused herself to go to the restroom; she thought they hardly seemed to notice. In the restroom she began to sob. She imagined that they were now exchanging phone numbers. How could they do this to her? How could they treat her this way? Why had she been so stupid as to invite Stacy to join them? But then, hadn't Eric really been the one to invite her? Had he immediately had his eye on her?

Returning to the table, Jane told Eric in a voice barely audible that she didn't feel well and would like to go home. He looked concerned and immediately reached for his wallet to take care of the bill while asking, "Are you all right?" "I just have a headache," Jane lied. They all stood up and Stacy began telling Jane how glad she was to see her again. Jane withheld eye contact and shuffled out of the restaurant. Eric tried to take her hand but she pulled away.

On the way home Jane was silent. Eric remarked about what an interesting job Stacy had; Jane thought he was making an excuse for his attentiveness. He also remarked about how fast and how much she talked. When Jane didn't respond, he asked her if something was wrong. Too devastated to answer, Jane began to cry silently. When they arrived home, Eric started to open his door but Jane told him he didn't need to get out; abruptly, she jumped out and hurried up the walk. She just wanted to get away from him.

Still awake hours later, Jane became even more depressed. What was wrong with her, she wondered, that she couldn't keep a man? She saw her future as lonely and desolate. She cried herself to sleep and called in sick the next morning, totally exhausted.

That day her thoughts raced as she started to get angry. First she blamed Stacy, then herself, then Eric. She began to imagine that Eric had only been spending time with her because he didn't have anyone else to date. She decided all his compliments had been lies, all his attention had been forced. She told herself she had been a fool to think he really cared. She told herself all men were the same; they couldn't be trusted.

Eric called Jane's work the next morning but was told she had called in sick; he called her at home but got no answer. That evening he drove straight to her home from work to see how she was feeling and to talk to her. With eyes swollen from crying, she opened the door and snapped, "What are you doing here?" Stunned, Eric mumbled, "I came to see you. Are you going to tell me what's wrong?" Jane attacked. "How could you treat me the way you did last night?" she screamed. "How dare you humiliate me like that? Have you called her for a date yet?" Eric stood there looking dumbfounded. "What are you talking about?" he demanded. "What did I do?" "You know exactly what you did," Jane exclaimed through her tears. "How dare you sit and flirt with my friend as though I didn't even exist. The two of you ignored me the whole evening." "We did not," Eric responded, "Where did you come up with this crazy idea, anyway? I was just trying to be nice to your friend."

When people with LSE experience a self-esteem attack, they display repetitive behaviors that form a Critical Incident Pattern. This 6-stage pattern begins with a specific incident that delivers a devastating blow to the person's self-esteem. As discussed in Chapter 3, this incident may not be one that would pose a threat or even create much of a reaction in a person with healthy self-esteem; however, it is one that proves devastating to the person with LSE. In the above example, Jane observed her boyfriend and her friend interacting in ways she interpreted as flirtatious and rude; this behavior became the critical incident that incited her humiliation and devastation. Whether or not her per-ceptions were true, Jane's reaction was to think that their behavior was an indictment of her—that she was unworthy in some way—and an indication that Eric was not the loyal person she thought he was, that she had been fooled in some way—another sign of her inadequacy. These are extreme conclusions to come to without discussion or further evidence, but Jane's LSE quickly ignites, often with less than normal provocation. When she becomes uncomfortable or threatened, her worst fears come to the forefront; she becomes irrational and blows the situation out of proportion.

The Stages of the Critical Incident Pattern:

1. The Critical Incident

2. Devastation

3. Anger

4. Scenario-Building

5. Confrontation

6. Return to Rationality

Stage 1: The Critical Incident

In Stage 1, a specific negative situation occurs without warning that upsets the person with LSE. This event may be the result of behaviors by another person, including criticism, a sarcastic remark, or a reprimand that the person with LSE experiences as rejection. For example, he is passed over for a promotion that he expected, he is denied a loan that was not in doubt, he is made the butt of a joke, or he is turned down for a date. Whatever the specifics, the cause of this critical incident is attributed to the actions of someone else.

This critical, triggering event, so upsetting to the person with LSE, may also be the result of the person's own behavior, perhaps doing poorly on a test, causing a traffic accident, burning the main dish shortly before company is to arrive, or saying something that afterwards they perceive to have been "stupid."

Stage 2: Devastation

In Stage 2, the individual quickly falls into an emotional whirlpool, feeling humiliated, depressed, despairing, or devastated. At this point, Quiet Reactors withdraw emotionally though they may be unable to do so physically without seemingly adding further embarrassment. Noisy Reactors may argue, become defensive, or blaming, attempting to cover their feelings.

Both make self-derogatory statements:

- Why can't I do anything right?

- I'm just a failure.

- I'm such a loser.

- I'm so worthless.

- I'm so pathetic.

This stage may last for a few minutes or extend for days, even weeks. As time progresses and the person has been unable to find her way out of this darkness, she begins to enlarge the scope of her self-condemnation with statements that predict the future:

- I've got to quit trying these things. I'll just keep failing.

- I'm never going to get a promotion.

- My partner is going to leave me and I'll be all alone.

- I'm never going to find someone who loves me.

- I'm never going to be able to do it right.

If the devastation lingers, the person may engage in self-abuse with food or other addictive behavior in an attempt to ease the growing anxiety and fear. Although he may realize he is overreacting, he will still be unable to recover from the depression that has overwhelmed him.

Unfortunately, he may even cancel his appointments with his therapist if he has one, too embarrassed to tell her of his most recent emotional fall, believing that no one can help him.

Stage 3: Anger

1. *Anger toward self*

Knowing that she is not handling the situation well only adds to the person's negative feelings about herself, propelling her into the anger stage. In this third stage, she rebukes herself asking "why" questions and whipping herself with "shoulds":

• Why am I so stupid? I should have known better.

• I should know enough to keep quiet.

• I should have just stayed home.

• I should have known he wouldn't want to go out with me.

• I should have known I wouldn't get the job.

• I should have known I wasn't smart enough to . . .

At this stage the person believes she "should have known," or she questions what is wrong with her that she "does not know" what she is sure that others do. Her awareness that she lacks the necessary skills only increases her fear and anxiety as she wonders how she will ever succeed in the world.

2. *Anger toward others*

In this stage, the person may also turn her anger toward someone else involved in the incident. Attempting to defend herself, she may fairly or unfairly blame the other person for treating her a certain way or simply encouraging her to participate. She may think that if her friend hadn't invited her to lunch, she wouldn't have had that auto accident while trying to get there. This, of course, is irrational thinking.

Sometimes the person with LSE will become enraged at the individual he perceives as sarcastic, unfair, teasing, or critical. Although this is a valid perception, the person with LSE, in his heightened irrational state, may exaggerate the importance or severity of the transgression. He may also attribute malicious intent to the other person's actions, as if the upsetting incident had been preplanned, purposely hurtful, even enjoyed. He may then overreact in this exaggeration by verbally attacking the other person; if he is a Quiet Reactor, he may detach or isolate.

Stage 4: Scenario-Building

Furthermore, the injured person may conclude that the actions of the one who has wounded him are a warning of something yet to come; he may be imagining, for example, that his partner, when she is rude or insensitive, is insinuating that she wants to end their relationship. He may believe that her actions indicate that she does not love or respect him. This first thought and the others that follow signal a move into the scenario stage, where the person with LSE builds a case against the "enemy." Analyzing and reanalyzing possible causes for her behavior, he convinces himself that the specific actions that hurt him are merely a sign of deeper problems.

He tells himself:

- She's so insensitive.

- She's so selfish.

- She doesn't really love me.

- She is taking advantage of me.

- She enjoys hurting me.

- She's making a fool out of me.

- She really wants out of our relationship.

- She's abusing me.

When he has accumulated enough evidence to support his negative beliefs, through vigilant observation and testing, the individual with LSE may return to the devastation stage and recycle through the anger stage. Or fueled with fury, he may move directly to Stage 5 and confront the other person with his conclusions.

Stage 5: Confrontation

The stage of confrontation is often confusing to people due to the irrationality of LSE.

- While going through a vulnerable period, the person with LSE vigilantly watches for a sign some one is being disloyal, laughing at her, disrespecting her, or mistreating her in some way. Because she is looking for such a gesture, she will probably find one, whether real or imagined, accurate or augmented.

- As a Noisy Reactor, the person with LSE will then aggressively confront and accuse her partner. Although she actually wants to be proven wrong, she is so deeply entrenched in her anger and fear that she cannot quiet her suspicions. She desperately wants her partner to see her pain, express his loyalty, and affirm her worth.

- Totally unaware of what she has been thinking and feeling, her partner is unprepared for this emotional outburst and the "documented" evidence that is presented. Unable to recognize her needs because he feels attacked, the partner gets "hooked" by her accusations, some of which may trigger his own insecurities, and then reacts with an angry defense. Or, if he is a Quiet Reactor himself, he may withdraw from her, further complicating the situation.

- The person with LSE who is already feeling extremely insecure and vulnerable may be further crushed by this response, perceiving that her partner is not responding to her pain. She feels she has completely exposed herself to him and he has responded in anger and criticism.

- If instead the partner can stay calm, recognizing that this is a self-esteem attack and a cry for love and acceptance, he may be able to give the person with LSE the reassurance she needs and the self-esteem attack and its aftermath can be halted. Incredibly, a simple statement may be enough. A statement validating her feelings and her experience, a word of apology, or an expression of love is all that's necessary to completely defuse this emotionally-loaded situation.

- People with LSE experience so much self-doubt that they frequently need reassurance that they are worthwhile and lovable individuals. Affirmation from her partner will calm her; she will then have the ability to see her exaggerations. Feeling relieved, though probably ashamed, she will revert back to a more rational state.

- If, however, the argument between them goes unresolved, it will take some other form of encouragement or affirmation to get the person with LSE out of this tailspin. This might come in the form of a compliment or support by another friend or co-worker—something to give the person a boost out of her negativity. (If she is a Quiet Reactor, she may simply withdraw and distance from the other person, skipping this stage of confrontation altogether, forcing the other person to pursue her to find out what the problem is.)

Stage 6: Return to Rationality

There comes a point at which the person with LSE becomes rational again after an episode of emotional reacting. This usually happens when he receives some affirmation from his significant other or when in the process of recovery, he learns to identify dysfunctional patterns of behavior and abort them himself. In this stage, he begins to see how he distorts facts, jumps to erroneous conclusions, and blames others inappropriately. If he can use this knowledge to recognize his pattern of distorting the truth, he can grow as a result; if he only whips himself with this insight, he will remain a slave to his low self-esteem.

RECOVERY

When a person understands the dysfunctional patterns of LSE, she can begin to recognize when she is in that cycle. Admitting to herself that she does indeed act in these ways is the first vital step towards change. If she can understand that these behaviors do not mean she is a bad person or a sick person but only that she is one of millions who act in these ways due to LSE, then maybe she can quit beating on herself and realize instead that she is actually making progress by acquiring this insight.

These LSE patterns do exist. They form a chain of dysfunction— a chain of low self-esteem that can be broken at any link. When the person with LSE becomes aware of the stage he is in, he can begin to talk himself out of that stage. He can learn to control his LSE rather than letting it control him.

Assertive, Passive, Aggressive, and Passive-Aggressive

People have a primary style in which they interact with others; this style becomes most pronounced during conflict. The four stances people take toward interactive conflict are assertiveness, passivity, aggression, or passive-aggression, though no one person acts in one definite style all of the time. For instance, many people find it relatively easy to be assertive at work, where the rules and expectations are more clearly defined, but they have difficulty maintaining assertiveness in their per-sonal relationships, where their emotions are so involved. A parent may be admired, respected, even lauded in the community where he is assertive yet become an aggressive monster at home with his children, or passive-aggressive in manipulating his wife to do his bidding. The following example, illustration, and discussion will elucidate these four styles of communication.

Example:

Richard and Judy both work outside the home: he for a graphic design company, she as a nurse. While together they have a reasonable income, their home mortgage and the expenses that accompany raising three children eat up most of their finances. They have tried to keep a small nest egg for emergencies and live a modest lifestyle.

In April, two months after having lost his job, Richard's brother, Jeff, came to him for a loan. After discussing the request with Judy, Richard explained to Jeff that the $5000 he had requested would nearly wipe out their small savings but that they would loan it to him if he agreed to begin making payments to them as soon as he found work. Jeff readily agreed, thanked them both, and said he didn't think it would take him long to land a new position. He offered to sign a note *and told them that he would make monthly payments of a least $250 beginning within 30 days of going back to work. Both Richard and Judy were pleased that he had suggested a specific plan to pay them back; they felt they could trust him and didn't think a note was necessary.*

Seven weeks later Richard heard from his mother that Jeff had found a job. Richard told Judy; they were both relieved. Jeff, however, did not call to tell them the news. They both felt it was somewhat inconsiderate on his part, but they were pleased he was back at work and could soon start paying back the loan.

Six more weeks went by and Jeff had still not called. At Judy's urging, Richard called Jeff to chat, hoping Jeff would bring up the loan; however, he did not. He also did not mention his new job and Richard felt awkward bringing it up himself. When they hung up, both Richard and Judy were uncomfortable.

Two more weeks went by and again Richard called Jeff. This time he was more direct and asked how the new job was going. Jeff hesitated and then said, "Great!" He added, "By the way, I've been going to call you. I figured Mom had told you about my job, but I wanted to talk to you about that loan I got from you." Richard was a little irritated but nonetheless relieved that Jeff was bringing up the subject of the loan. He was taken aback, however, when he heard Jeff continue to say, "I'm not going to be able to start the payments as quickly as I'd hoped but I want you to know that I am planning on paying you back. I just hope you can be patient with me a little longer as I got behind on some things during those weeks I was out of work. I'll be caught up soon though and then I can start sending you checks."

What could Richard say? Obviously, Jeff couldn't make the payments if he didn't have the money, and he did say it wouldn't be long before he'd be caught up. He said to Jeff, "I wish you had called me, Jeff. You didn't even call to let us know you had found work and I wonder if you would have even talked to me about the delay if I hadn't initiated this call. "Of course, I would have," responded Jeff, irritably. "You sound like you don't trust me. In fact, I was going to call you this afternoon." Richard wondered if that was the truth but didn't say more. Jeff said he was really busy and needed to go, so they hung up.

The following evening Richard and Judy invited Richard's mother out to dinner. They had not told her about the loan they had made to Jeff but were curious to get her assessment of his new job; they were hoping it paid enough that Jeff would actually be able to make the payments they had all agreed upon. As dinner progressed, Richard casually brought up Jeff and told his mother that he had talked to Jeff recently. Before he could ask her about his work, she blurted out, "Did he tell you he bought a new sports car?" Richard's mouth dropped open; Judy just stared, first at his mother, then at Richard. His mother was still talking. "I don't understand how he thinks he can possibly afford expensive car payments after being out of work for several weeks." Richard didn't know what to say but felt Judy kick him under the table. Both could hardly wait for the meal to be over so they could talk to one another about Jeff. His mother seemed not to notice their responses.

Figure 6: Passive, Aggressive, Assertive, Passive-Aggressive

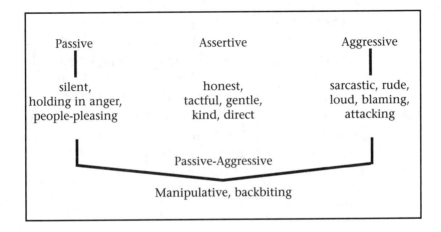

Assertive

Learning to be assertive is essential to overcoming low self-esteem and it is critical to forming healthy relationships; assertiveness entails being honest and direct while also being tactful, gentle, and kind in the process. When we are assertive, we are willing to be vulnerable by saying what we actually think and feel; this is a choice we make. When someone hurts or upsets us, we take the risk of confronting that person about his behavior. We confront in a gentle and kind manner because the purpose is to correct the behavior, not to offend in return. We approach the person as tactfully as possibly because the intent is to heal, not wound.

Being assertive is risky because the person being approached may get angry or may reject us as a result. The assertive person knows, however, that it is worth the risk because being assertive means being willing to be honest and open, allowing an opportunity for the relationship to grow and develop. A relationship built on anything other than assertiveness is not an honest relationship but one built on manipulation, fear, and/or control.

It is impossible to have a truly intimate relationship without being assertive, because intimacy is a closeness with someone that is based on honesty, openness, trust, and willingness to be vulnerable. People can be physically intimate in a relationship but not have achieved emotional intimacy (this is actually the condition of many marriages and other committed relationships). A healthy, truly intimate relationship requires that the level of physical interaction not go beyond that of the emotional level of interaction. Thus, a relationship in which two people are physically intimate but only acquaintances will be a very poor overall relationship, though the couple may enjoy their sexual activity. In the reverse, however, it is, of course, possible to be emotionally intimate without physical intimacy. Friendships that focus on assertive, open interaction often develop healthy intimacy, while romantic relationships that do not foster assertiveness do not.

Assertive behavior is best, not only for the relationship, but also for each person individually; neither is required to "swallow" feelings or repress anger and each one knows where he stands with the other.

In the above example, if Richard decided to be assertive he would confront calmly and tactfully. Knowing it's appropriate to deal with anger by going to the source, he would risk alienating Jeff, realizing that honesty is best for each of them and best for the relationship. His purpose would be twofold: to get rid of his anger and, more importantly, to repair a relationship that has been compromised.

Passive

The majority of people in our culture are passive; our society has conditioned them to be afraid to speak out and share their opinions. Instead, they hold in their true feelings; they do not stand up for themselves or speak in their own defense, remaining silent while others abuse and misuse them. They may let others take credit for their work or project blame on to them with nary a reply. Quietly accepting what comes their way, they do not ask their boss for a much deserved raise, or they may put up with a partner who mistreats them. With a basic don't-rock-the-boat mentality, passive people also criticize and punish others who attempt to be assertive, silencing their attempts to be honest. The fact that others usually do not encourage assertiveness makes it even more acceptable to choose to be passive.

When being honest about their passivity, people often state that "they don't say anything" or "don't speak up" because they don't want to hurt anyone's feelings. While this may be true in part, more often the real reason is a fear of rejection, a fear that others will not approve or like them if they dare to be honest. Passivity is usually an attempt to please others in order to be accepted, and it requires a willingness to compromise ourselves in the process. Unwilling to be honest and direct, the passive person gives up his right to his own opinions and wishes, choosing to defer to others instead.

Choosing to be passive to protect another's feelings is not only harmful to the other person but is demeaning as well. Making such a choice says to the other person, "I won't tell you how I feel. I don't believe that you are capable of dealing with reality. You are too fragile. I must protect you."

Inaccurately believing that confrontation or honesty is wrong or too risky, passive people live trying to "keep the peace" to the detriment of their own mental and physical health. It is well known that holding in our feelings causes stress that can result in headaches, anxiety, and other health problems; yet those who practice passivity as a lifestyle make choices based on the pressures of the moment, ignoring the long-range effects this may have on them.

Unfortunately, assertiveness is not generally considered the most appropriate behavior and it is not usually rewarded. Instead, people are often punished for telling the truth, for expressing their feelings, and for making individual choices. Consequently, people are afraid to tell their bosses what they think for fear of retaliation; they are equally fearful of confronting their spouses. Rather than be assertive, friends tolerate inappropriate behavior and are left feeling uncomfortable about the relationship, guilty that they have been dishonest, yet too fearful of the alternative. Passive people then live with the uncertainty of not knowing where they stand with others, unable to broach the subject, unsure of how the other feels.

Passivity creates dishonest relationships. To be passive is a choice that prevents true intimacy by creating distance through uncertainty; it also limits the potential of those involved by depriving them of honest feedback and reliable input.

Passivity is destructive to relationships in another way as well. Most people who practice passive behavior have anger that wells up within them over time. Then, much like the contents of a cup filled beyond capacity, that anger cannot be contained but overflows, usually at inopportune and unfortunate times. Unlike the overflow from the cup, however, the force with which this anger escapes resembles a volcanic eruption; with pressure from within, the entire reservoir of hurt and resentment explodes onto its unsuspecting target. Thus every few weeks or months, the passive person will blow up and "dump" on someone, guiltily returning to passive behavior when this storm has abated. (The difference between the aggressive person and this passive person is that aggression is consistently the response of the first, and only occasionally the behavior of the second, who has been storing up resentments. More people with LSE fall into this mode of passivity than any of the other three ways of responding to conflict.

If Richard chose to be passive about the situation between them and Jeff, he would do nothing, telling himself that talking to Jeff would only make things worse. Without realizing it, he would place it in his personal video where it would be ready for instant replay. He would continue to have contact with Jeff but would not mention his feelings of betrayal or that he knew about the sports car. Jeff's actions, however, would eat at Richard; at a later time, when he is furious about Jeff's unpaid loan or some other totally unrelated incident, he might blurt out his angry feelings to Jeff.

Aggressive

Aggressive behavior is criticized more often than passive behavior; its destructive consequences are more readily apparent, making it easier to recognize. We may not know when someone is being passive, but we can immediately identify aggressive behaviors such as pushing, shouting, hitting, or throwing things. Other forms of aggressive behavior include bullying, blaming, demeaning others, sarcasm, ridicule, and forcefully attempting to control.

While passivity is encouraged, society frowns on aggressive behavior, yet each is equally destructive, one merely being more visible than the other. For this reason, aggressive people are more likely to curb their assaults in public settings, such as their job, while reverting back to the destructive behavior in their private lives.

Although those with LSE are often labeled as aggressive because of their incessant confrontations and outbursts, their behaviors are more often the result of the stored-up anger and consequent explosions of the passive person. A few, however, are actually aggressive as their initial response.

People with LSE may exhibit aggressive behavior due to the inner rage they carry with them from abuse. Feeling misunderstood, disrespected, and unimportant, they may explode in frustration; this behavior is even more likely if they experience a situation similar to the ways they were mistreated in the past. Sadly, those who have been abused by aggressive parents or other authority figures often replicate the kind of discipline or punishment they observed and experienced by treating their children in this same way.

Richard could call up Jeff and yell at him on the phone or drive over to his house and display his anger in Jeff's presence. He could verbally attack Jeff, threaten to beat him up, and slam the door as he leaves. He could sarcastically berate Jeff. These would all be aggressive responses.

Passive-aggressive

Passive-aggressive is an interaction style all its own and should not be confused with those who are primarily passive or primarily aggressive. A combination of the two, passive-aggressive behavior takes place when a person acts "directly" passive to the person while acting "indirectly" aggressive. For example, Richard may not tell Jeff that he is angry with him (passive), but he may tell others what a jerk he is (aggressive). In this way, he hurts Jeff indirectly by making others think less of him, while he acts passively in Jeff's presence.

Other forms of passive-aggressive behavior include any form of manipulation, deliberate tardiness, pouting (which is meant to make the other person feel bad), and any action intended to figuratively "stab the other person in the back." Because it is the most deceptive response mode, it is the most difficult to detect, and certainly the most troublesome to prove.

Passive-aggressive behavior is the most destructive of the communication styles; people dealing with passive-aggressive individuals continually experience feelings of confusion and rage. Masters of manipulation and deceit, passive-aggressive people are able to fool casual friends and acquaintances, who often sing their praises and come to their defense, further confusing those who deal regularly with these problem people. On the surface, they may be charming and fun but when they want something badly, they will go to any length to reach their goal. They tend to be extremely untrustworthy and use their passive-aggressive interactions to cover their irresponsible behavior.

Passive-aggressive behavior is common among those with LSE. Afraid to be assertive or to openly display their hostility, they resort to this means of indirectly acting out their anger at others; their feelings may have long been ignored or discounted and they know no other way to get their needs met or to express their intense pain; they also may wish to retaliate. Quiet Reactors use this method of communication even more than Noisy Reactors, who are somewhat more prone to aggressive behavior, though they, too, are frequently passive-aggressive.

If Richard chose to respond to Jeff in a passive-aggressive manner, he could:

- not talk to Jeff, but call up their mother and possibly other relatives instead, telling them what Jeff had done.

- tell Jeff's girlfriend about his behavior.

- manipulate Jeff in some way.

- make snide remarks about Jeff to others, in Jeff's presence.

- ask Jeff to do something for him with some promise of compensation and then never pay him, hoping Jeff would learn his lesson from the experience.

- *A note of comparison with those with healthy self-esteem:*

Healthy people act in assertive ways most of the time. They openly and directly share their opinions and ideas in appropriate ways. When hurt or angry, they express these feelings. Though they are not perfect communicators, they do not hold back their thoughts or feelings or passively protect their loved ones from the truth; they seldom act in aggressive ways; they rarely punish others passive- aggressively. They want the best for themselves and others and know the only way to have healthy relationships is by being honest, open, and direct.

RECOVERY

Assertiveness is the only healthy way to respond and behave in life. To become assertive, one must first believe that it is the appropriate mode of communication. Deciding to become an assertive person is a quantum leap toward recovery from low self-esteem. Only through assertive behavior can we work through our anger and pain.

This may or may not lead us to go back and confront people from our past who have been hurtful to us. Those situations must be looked at individually. Becoming an assertive person, however, does mean making a commitment to start today to make conscious choices to act assertively.

THINGS TO DO

During the course of their lives, people use all four of the distinct relational styles, but they have one to which they subscribe the most in their interpersonal relationships, especially in times of conflict. It is important, therefore, to learn to recognize these patterns both in yourself and others.

1. Read through the definitions of assertive, passive, aggressive, and passive-aggressive until you have a clear understanding of each.

2. Each day, watch for one example of each type of behavior in the interactions around you. This may be in communication between your family members, between you and someone else, between coworkers, or even on television. What's important is that you find the examples, not where you find them.

3. Write these examples down in your notebook.

4. Go over the definitions again to be sure you have classified your examples correctly.

5. Do this exercise daily for four weeks. By then, you will be very familiar with each pattern of behavior and you will be able to recognize and identify your own verbal behavior as you work toward becoming an assertive person.

Were you surprised to identify that you are passive, aggressive, or even passive-aggressive much of the time? Don't be discouraged. Since you have probably not been encouraged to be assertive, you have latched onto one of the other communication styles in order to cope. When you feel you can, begin experimenting with more assertive responses. Take your time; you can't do this overnight. Applaud yourself when you are successful in being assertive and write it in your notebook.

10

Empowered to Build
a New Life

JANE: therapy and change

When Jane had been in therapy for about nine months, she began to realize how much she was truly changing, how different her life was beginning to be, how exciting the future might be. Looking back, she could see the subtle and not-so-subtle ways in which her thinking was becoming different now, her responses were new, and her emotions were more moderate. She was truly developing attitudes that were foreign to her past—and she was elated. In the past week, her therapist had told Jane she was really making progress.

In thinking of specific situations, Jane—

- *Recognized she had responded in a much healthier fashion when she was asked to join the company walk-a-thon, and had been able to participate without excessive anxiety.*

- *Laughed as she realized she had conquered her fear of parallel parking since she had gotten the courage to ask an older neighbor to teach her. They had spent several evenings practicing right in front of her home. He had told her that parallel parking is a learned skill and that most people aren't very good at it because they avoid it rather than practicing the maneuver.*
- *Shook her head remembering the times she had decided to quit therapy and had even canceled some sessions, thinking her therapist must be getting tired of her continual failures and depression. Fortunately, she had gone back.*

- *Smiled as she remembered the vice president of her company asking her if she could handle the position of department head and her confident reply that she not only thought she could handle it but that he would not be sorry he had promoted her.*

- *Felt proud when she realized that she had assertively confronted her present male companion when he insinuated that she should cut back on her activities to spend more time with him. Pointing out that he was expecting her to fit her life around his while she hadn't seen him making any such sacrifices had felt good. He had been surprised but had actually agreed that she was right and that his expectations had been unfair.*

- *Was pleased with the fact that she was beginning to set boundaries with her mother, though this was probably the most difficult task that she had to do. It was at least a beginning.*

- *Could see that she was more comfortable in public since she had set a goal to go out once a week by herself to a movie, dinner, shopping, art gallery, etc. Her therapist had encouraged her to hold her head up, to look around at other people, to take an interest in her surroundings, in essence to get her mind off herself while on these outings.*

Feeling more content then she could ever remember, Jane was well aware that there were still difficult times as well. While her periods of devastation and depression were less frequent and shorter, they were still occurring; and while her self-state-ments weren't always negative, they continued to be a serious problem. Her fear of failure was certainly still lurking nearby, but she was beginning to see how irrational her thinking was. Hey! She was making progress, wasn't she? That's what counted. She was beginning to understand and identify her self-defeating behaviors though sometimes after the fact; she hadn't totally conquered her problems yet. Yet. That was the word. She just hadn't conquered them "yet."

Like others who have struggled to overcome low self-esteem, Jane did not experience her entire life changing overnight. Instead she soon learned that such change in a person's life is sel-dom dramatic; it is a process, often dull, often tedious. She began to understand that this was a life transition, and that in order to change from a caterpillar to a butterfly, she would have to be patient, taking one step at a time. Embarking on this new adven-ture, she would eventually find her true self and grow to appreciate who she was; she was learning to rejoice in each sign that indicated movement toward that transformation.

The Process of Change

Change can take place; change is possible for each of us. We can modify our rigid views, we can alter our self-defeating habits, we can learn new skills—and there are specific steps to accom-plishing these goals.

The following stages apply to any and all areas of change:

- *Awareness:* The first step to developing any new skill, altering any specific behavior pattern, and ultimately making permanent change is that of becoming aware—both of the need for that change and the means to that change, e.g., a golfer who continually slices the ball will be aware that she needs to do something differently, whether it be to adjust her stance, her swing, or her grip. She may not know where the problem lies, but she will recognize there is a problem. She will have a general awareness that change is necessary.

- *Analysis:* Once an initial awareness is present, the next step is to hone that awareness. As with a microscope, we must now study or analyze the individual elements to discern where the problem lies, a process that will provide further insight and a more finely tuned awareness. For example, you may have questioned whether you have LSE; you may have even recognized that you do. You have a general awareness of it. To further figure out your dilemma, you may have purchased this book to get more information—so that you can analyze your problem in more depth. As a result of reading this book, you now have additional insight about how your low self-esteem developed, how it affects your life, and how you sabotage your own goals because of that negative view of self. This is good. This is progress. You have expanded your awareness.

  Now you may want to discuss this with a friend, your partner, or a family member. You may want to enter therapy or begin to work on the problem on your own. To do that, you will need to set goals and develop a plan. Feeling overwhelmed? Then remember that the trick to working on any new skill is to continue breaking it down into smaller pieces until each step seems manageable. If your plan still seems beyond reach, then make smaller goals.

1. Target goal: Recover from Low Self-Esteem

2. Important First Steps that must be worked on throughout recovery:

   - Work on recognizing distorted thinking

   - Work on altering distorted thinking

   - Work on practicing correct thinking

3. The second step consists of self-defeating behaviors to be worked on one by one (Note: These are intended as examples only. List your own.)

   - Inability to spend time alone

   - Dependence on others

   - Overly self-conscious

   - Avoidance of specific problems

   - Avoidance of social situations

   - Poor communication skills

   - Lack of hobbies or interests

   - Lack of a support group

   - Unfamiliarity with my own feelings

   - Problems with anger

- Inability to make friends

- Lack of assertiveness

4. Choose one from your list above. (Example: lack of assertiveness)

5. List all the possible things you feel you could do to work on the self-defeating behavior you have chosen. These are process goals.

Examples:

- Take a class on assertiveness.

- Attend a workshop on assertiveness.

- Read a book on assertiveness.

- Discuss assertiveness with a friend.

- Go to therapy.

- Begin watching the behavior of others.

- Attempt one assertive behavior daily.

6. Choose one process goal (above) and make a plan for working on this goal by setting even smaller goals. For example:

- I will make a list of things I could do to work on being more assertive and try one new one each week.

- I will work each day on trying to be more assertive until I become more comfortable.

- I will read a book on assertiveness.

- I will go to the library Thursday evening.

- I will ask the librarian to help me find books on assertiveness.
- I will check out one book on the subject.

- I will spend one hour three days a week reading this book.

- I will begin writing down my new insights in a note book.

- *Practice:* New insights remain just that—insights—unless we put them into practice. This need to practice cannot be overemphasized. Everything we do well, we have practiced. We were not born with the ability to use a computer, ride a bicycle, play tennis, or even walk, let alone be assertive. We were not born knowing how to brush our teeth, how to give a speech, or how to develop relationships. If you now do not know how to do something, this is simply because you have not yet learned this skill and/or have not practiced it sufficiently. Not knowing how to do something does not mean you are incapable of learning it—you merely haven't learned it yet. While it may be embarrassing to think you are just now learning how to relate to others or are just now learning to be independent, try to remember that you are the product of your environment—you obviously were never taught this skill or given sufficient opportunity or encouragement to practice. This occurs for many reasons that are not your fault.

In addition to being deprived of the instruction and other influences that would have enabled us to develop skills, most of us have also been conditioned to avoid practicing certain skills. Such is the case with assertiveness skills discussed in Chapter 9. Society frowns on assertive behavior and often punishes those who display such direct interaction. Ultimately, regardless of why we are now unskilled in any area of our lives, this merely means we haven't learned that skill yet. We may not be assertive now, but we can learn to be so, if we practice. Try to focus on how to learn this skill rather than berating yourself for not having attained it already. Focus on the future—moving forward—not on the past.

- *Feedback:* An important aspect of learning new behaviors is receiving feedback. As we begin practicing new behaviors, we want to be sure we are learning those new behaviors correctly. The person who is attempting to improve her golf shot will want to have her instructor observe her from time to time so she can be sure she is correcting her deficiencies and not developing additional bad tendencies.

  In trying to develop assertiveness, it will be most helpful to have a friend or partner who is also striving to attain that skill or who is already an assertive person. You can then give each other feedback, share observations, and support each other. Group therapy can also provide an excellent environment in which to receive constructive feedback when we are learning and trying out relational skills.

- *Integration:* The goal, of course, is to be able to utilize these new skills in our daily lives, to become more confident, self-respecting, self-loving, and self-nurturing. As self-esteem improves, we will be able to believe in ourselves, feel good about ourselves, and feel worthy, adequate, and competent.

- *Patience:* Try to be patient with yourself and the process. Your view of yourself and your LSE has developed over your entire life. You can temporarily change behaviors quickly, but this type of change doesn't last—it's merely a behavior change.

Permanent change requires that your thinking and attitude readjust, that they go through a process of being permanently modified, and this takes time—there are no shortcuts.

Severely low self-esteem is complex. While everyone with low self-esteem does not respond in exactly the same way in any given situation, all people with LSE participate to some degree in the basic principles described here. Those with only mild low self-esteem may never have felt extreme devastation or they may have experienced it less often. Though they may not recognize it, all those with LSE at times experience fear and anxiety and perform self-defeating behaviors. Nearly all find that this struggle with LSE negatively impacts their relationships and daily lives.

As you have read through these ideas, you may have seen yourself in the examples. Try not to be embarrassed; you have not been publicly exposed; you are the only one who really knows your problems.

I hope that if you are among those who live with LSE, you now understand how it works, where it came from, and that you can begin your journey out of its clutches. I caution you, however, that most people cannot overcome LSE without assistance and encourage you to consider therapy.

Why the Need for Therapy?

In working through the complicated issues of LSE, we each need someone who can:

1. Remain objective in the midst of our confusion.

   Remaining objective is extremely difficult when we are examining aspects of our own lives. In the beginning, the pitfalls are not obvious and an accurate self-assessment of our actions or expectations will be unrealistic. Clarification and help from another source such as a therapist can provide a more accurate perspective that will then inspire insight into the complexities of LSE.

2.   Confront us assertively, when it's appropriate to do so.

Unfortunately, those of us with LSE have likely formed certain rigid patterns of thinking and responding that are not in our best interest. Consequently, at times we may need to be confronted about these departures from the truth. Trained therapists have the skills to do this in a sensitive manner; they are able to challenge us and intervene at the appropriate times when we plunge into denial or perform repetitive self-defeating behaviors. In time, we will have an arsenal of strategies to use in recognizing our irrational and self-destructive patterns; in the beginning, however, we will be unable to generalize from one situation to another. We will need to rely on the expertise of someone more objective and informed to point out these errors while suggesting reasonable alternative behaviors.

3.   Encourage us and point out our progress.

The issues of LSE are extremely convoluted and confusing as shown below:

- Our irrational perceptions invoke specific illogical fears.

- These fears propel us toward self-destructive behaviors.

- This action generates remorse and self-recrimination.

- Self-recrimination invokes more negative perceptions of self.

- These links form the chain and stimulate the cycle to continue.

Too entrenched in the problem to be able to sort out the intricacies of this interwoven pattern, we will be equally blind to recognizing our progress as we initially take steps toward changing. A therapist who does not share this negative perspective and whose vision is not clouded by the magnitude of the problem will be able to point out the subtle but significant modifications we are making in our lives. When we become impatient and discouraged because progress seems slow or nonexistent, the therapist will be able to encourage us and assure us that we are definitely heading in the right direction and at a reasonable pace, by pointing out the specific changes we have made, the insights we have shared, and the results that we have achieved to that point. Having someone to give us this feedback concerning the steps of growth that we have taken is so important because those of us suffering from LSE are quick to criticize ourselves and to invalidate our progress.

4.   Demonstrate continuous respect.

When we suffer from LSE, we also suffer from damaged self-respect. Engaging in a therapeutic relationship with someone who treats people with unwavering respect is therefore critical to the healing process. Such a relationship enables a person to consistently encounter an attitude that she may never have experienced before, one that enhances her view of herself and says that she is worthy and deserving. This relationship will serve as a model of the appropriate way to view herself.

The process of change is always an undulating one. We may feel we are making progress for a week, then feel like we have taken a step backward. Some days we may feel that we are growing and changing by leaps and bounds; other days we might feel both discouraged and defeated. At these times, the respectful comments of the therapist can help get us back on track, help us shake off our negativism, and give us hope.

Moods fluctuations during this transition period may be turbulent. At times, we may think we have the vision; we may believe in ourselves and be excited about the future. Later the same day or week, we may decide we are totally confused and that the future is bleak. This is a typical reaction for anyone working through issues of LSE. Respect from the therapist will go a long way toward motivating the person at this point in recovery.

The need for support, encouragement, direction, and feedback are not unique to people with LSE. They are critical requirements for anyone working through any serious personal problem and are important to living healthy lives. Those with LSE who are just beginning to face their problem, however, are less likely to have these resources outside of therapy. They are unlikely to have quality close relationships, they may feel too vulnerable to share their problems with others, they may have poor social skills and be unable to relate on this level, and they may view themselves as beyond help.

How to Choose a Therapist

Note: It is highly recommended that before choosing a therapist you first read *Low Self-Esteem: Misunderstood & Misdiagnosed: Why You May Not Find the Help You Need* by Marilyn J Sorensen, PhD (Wolf, 2001).

When selecting a therapist, prepare questions and interview several. Remember the following:

• Only engage in therapy with a person who thoroughly understands the problems of low self-esteem and who specializes in working with these issues. Many therapists do not. When searching for the right counselor, ask her how she works on this issue. Ask what she sees to be the significant elements of LSE. If she cannot articulate the main points in this book (how LSE forms, the role of fear and anxiety in LSE, the emotional trauma it causes, and the self-sabotaging patterns that then control the persons life), call someone else.

- Your therapist should also be a "teaching" therapist—one who is prepared to teach you new skills, offer guidance, make suggestions, and provide explanations. Ask your potential therapist in what ways he participates in the sessions. If he states that he only listens, this will not be adequate. If he adds to that that he asks questions and gives feedback, this, too, will be insufficient. Keep looking. You need someone who is able to explain skills in detail and who can instruct you in acquiring those skills.

- Do not expect therapy to feel too comfortable. Sharing your fear, anxiety, self-defeating behaviors, and emotional turmoil will make you feel vulnerable. Your past hypervigilance will cause you to be on guard and "uptight."

- Be prepared. Your therapist may need to confront you at times and this may be difficult to handle. Try to remember that a therapist who will be open, direct, and honest with you is exactly what you need, if it is accompanied by compassion, understanding, and— above all—respect.

- If you are convinced you have low self-esteem, do not remain in therapy if your therapist tries to steer you in a different direction. Many may try to work on your accompanying depression, decide you simply need anger management training, or want to work on some other such symptom of LSE instead of addressing the problem of low self-esteem directly. (While it may be true that you need to work on anger or other problems, this should come either during or after your work on self-esteem. *They are not the core issues.*)

- If your therapist talks about "raising your self-esteem" rather than "recovering from it," beware. This therapist does not really understand low self-esteem, for you either have LSE or you don't. Some may have it more severely, but most therapists don't understand that low self-esteem is a thought disorder— you either see yourself in a negative light in segments of your life or you see yourself in a positive light in every aspect of your life (healthy self-esteem). Consequently, as a person who suffers from LSE, your goal in going to therapy is to find someone who belives that you can "overcome" this problem through a process of recovery.

- Try not to become discouraged in your process of recovery. If you are in therapy, do not cancel or avoid appointments when you are devastated or upset or embarrassed. This is the time you most need to see your therapist.

- After your initial period of therapy, it is advisable to involve a loved one (whether friend, family member, or partner) to serve as your "midwife" in this rebirthing process. In other words, it would be helpful to have one of these people actually attend your sessions with you. Do not include someone, however, unless you highly trust them and perceive them as positive and supportive. If your therapist does not recognize the need for this, consider moving on to a different therapist.

- Recognize that the process of improving self-esteem is a long-term undertaking. Do not expect instant relief and try not to evaluate each session. Only after weeks and months of therapy will you be able to look back and clearly perceive your progress, although your therapist will be able to point out intermediate steps that you may not have noticed.

- Commit yourself to a *minimum* of a year in therapy. Any therapist who suggests that you will be able to solve this problem in less time does not possess a thorough understanding of the complexities of the issues involved. When first interviewing therapists, ask if they do long-term or short-term therapy—there are different skills involved in each. Only someone trained and accustomed to doing long-term therapy can meet your needs.

- Do not remain in therapy with someone who does not give you positive feedback. You will need a lot of encouragement and support in this process.

- Do not remain in therapy with a therapist who is unsupportive or critical, or who minimizes your emotional experiences. You've already had enough criticism—you don't need to pay someone to give you more.

- Being able to afford therapy is a problem for many people; it is indeed expensive. Remember, however, that it is an investment in your future and may well affect the rest of your life more than any new endeavor you consider. People sometimes take on a second job, take money from savings, borrow from family members, or forego vacations to make this commitment.

- Group therapy is often more affordable than individual therapy and can be a very worthwhile option if financial obstacles would otherwise prohibit you from getting the help you need.

REMEMBER

You have within you the ability to alter the situation you are now in and the emotions that you now experience. You may not have received the guidance and support you needed in your youth to learn the skills you now lack; however, this deficiency can be overcome. Not having a skill does not mean you are unable to learn the skill. You can do it now. With support, perseverance, determination, and a vision for a better life, you can break the chain that now enslaves you in misery—but you must do it one day at a time and one link at a time. You must also be determined, persistent, and unrelenting in your pursuit of recovery from this devastating problem—low self-esteem. You can do it. I have guided hundreds of people through recovery and I know that it is achievable. Whether you engage in therapy or not, set goals for yourself, work on the exercises in this book, chart your progress, and then make positive self-statements about your successes.

Índex

Marilyn J Sorensen, PhD, is a clinical psychologist in Portland, Oregon and the founder and director of the Self-Esteem Institute. A leading expert in self-esteem recovery work, Dr. Sorensen conducts phone therapy and consultation with people worldwide.

To contact the author:

Dr. Sorensen welcomes your comments and will answer one question per reader at no charge.

Phone: 503-330-2830
Email: mjsorensen@GetEsteem.com

COMING IN 2007:

Dr. Sorensen is presently working on an important and exciting new book that more thoroughly explains her theory of self-esteem and her recovery program. The book illustrates why the process of attempting to "raise self-esteem" doesn't transform low self-esteem into healthy self-esteem and is therefore of little value.

Information in this new book will completely alter thinking and understanding of low self-esteem, likely influencing all future therapy approaches for recovery from low self-esteem and hopefully becoming the first step toward the rightful inclusion of "Low self-esteem" in the APA Diagnostic Manual as a disorder rather than simply a symptom of other disorders.

To order more copies:

Go to: www.TheSelfEsteemInstitute.com

Call: 503-625-1545

Write: Wolf Publishing Co.
16890 SW Daffodil St.
Sherwood, OR 97140

WE OFFER DISCOUNTS ON ALL ORDERS
AND FREE SHIPPING WITHIN THE U.S.

Ebook edition of this book only available through
www.TheSelfEsteemInstitute.com or www.GetSelfEsteem.com

Trade paper edition also available through bookstores nationwide.

Other Books by Dr. Marilyn J. Sorensen

*Breaking the Chain of Low Self-Esteem......*1998

*Low Self-Esteem: Misunderstood & Misdiagnosed......*2001

*The Personal Workbook for Breaking the Chain of Low Self-Esteem......*2002

*The Handbook for Building Healthy Self-Esteem in Children......*2003

*Low Self-Esteem in the Bedroom: How LSE affects Intimacy.....*2004

*The Personal Workbook for Breaking the Chain of Low Self-Esteem- Ebook version......*2005

*Breaking the Chain of Low Self-Esteem (Newly Revised Edition)- Ebook version......*2006

*Low Self-Esteem: Misunderstood & Misdiagnosed Ebook version......*2006

*The Handbook for Building Healthy Self-Esteem in Children Ebook version......*2006

*Low Self-Esteem in the Bedroom: How LSE affects Intimacy Ebook version.....*2006

*Romper las Cadenas de la Baja Autoestima (Breaking the Chain of Low Self-Esteem in Spanish)......*2006

101 Great Ways to Improve Your Life, (Dr. Sorensen is a co-author)......2006

Other Resources

*The Self-Esteem Recovery Toolkit......*2002